Careers for Women in Uniform

Careers
for Women
in Uniform

by GROVER HEIMAN, Jr.,
Col., USAF (Ret.)

and VIRGINIA HEIMAN MYERS

J. B. Lippincott Company

PHILADELPHIA / NEW YORK

DEDICATED TO *Viva Williamson*

Contents

Careers for Women in Uniform

Introduction

This can truly be called the Age of the Atom, but also there is another revolution and it is called the Age of the Woman. She has been emancipated in the twentieth century and has gained equality in many areas long considered the private domain of men. In the past thirty years the emergence of women in society is as astounding as that of splitting the atom, and in the long run is going to have more effect on life on our planet than that great discovery.

The Department of Labor has this to say about woman-power:

"Womanpower is one of our country's greatest resources. Women's skills and abilities are being used more fully and more creatively than ever before—in the home, in the community, and on the job.

"Since 1940 American women have been responsible for the major share in the growth of the labor force. They account for more than 60 percent of the total increase from 1940 to 1964, and their representation in the labor force has risen from one-fourth to more than one-third of all workers.

"The growing contribution made by women to the economic life of the country has developed largely as a result of many social and economic changes of the last twenty-five years. Women have been freed for work outside the home by scientific and technological advances that have simplified home chores. The growth of new industries in a dynamic economy and expanded activities in others, as in commerce and trade, have opened new doors for women in business, the professions, and the production of goods and services.

"The increased demand for women as workers has been accompanied by broadened opportunities for their education and by girls' and women's increased awareness of the need for more training. The great emphasis in recent years on completion of high school, on occupational training, on university education, and on continuing education for mature women has encouraged women to seek better preparation for jobs. This has facilitated their integration into the working world."

One of the most promising ways for a young woman to gain training and further education is through service in the armed forces of the United States. The Army, Navy, Marine Corps, and Air Force provide that training and also offer the opportunity for a lifetime career in uniform.

This book explores the opportunities for careers in the armed forces for women.

Grover Heiman, Jr., Col., USAF (Ret.)
Virginia H. Myers

CHAPTER 1

From Then to Now

Throughout the centuries, women of all nations have courageously defended their homes and homelands. Many have given their lives. In the past the military profession has not accepted women because of the physical demands, but today that has changed dramatically because many jobs are technical in nature and women can do them as well, and often better than men. The actual job of fighting, however, is still reserved for men, as it has always been.

Yet historians recount many heroic stories of women who had to fight alongside their men in order to survive. In this country, during the early colonial days, hardy pioneer women often fought marauding Indians. In later conflicts and wars there were some brave women who posed as men to fight for country or cause. But it was not until after the turn of the twentieth century that women were granted suffrage and the right to wear the uniform of their country.

This did not, however, dampen their patriotism. One of the early American patriots was Margaret Corbin, better known as "Captain Molly."

During the Revolutionary War she fought beside her husband with the Continental Army against the British Redcoats. When he was wounded by the British at the Battle of Fort Washington, she took over his cannon. She defied the fire of the onrushing British until she too fell wounded. For her heroism, General George Washington awarded her the rank of sergeant. On July 6, 1779, she was pensioned by the Continental Congress. Captain Molly now rests at West Point beneath a memorial statue dedicated to her role in history.

Early in the Revolutionary War, General Washington recognized the need for military nursing, which then was a very rudimentary science. He recruited women and paid his nurses a salary of ten dollars a month, including room and board. Even though their duties were little more than distributing food and water, he realized the necessity for battlefield nurses.

There were other heroines of the Revolutionary War, such as Deborah Sampson Gannet, who, disguised as a man, enlisted in the Continental Army. She was wounded twice and each time denied herself medical treatment because of fear of discovery. She was subsequently detected, received an honorary discharge from the Army and was pensioned as an invalid soldier.

After the Revolutionary War, and through the days of the Mexican War, women often accompanied their husbands on military operations. In 1846, for example, Sarah Borginis gained fame for her bravery during an Indian attack at Fort Brown, Texas. General Scott bestowed on her the rank of colonel for her exploits. When she died in 1866 she received a military funeral.

The patriotic spirit flourished strongly during the Civil War. To a great extent it was because women were the guiding force to abolish slavery. A surprising number of women served in both the Union and Confederate armies, each sincere in their beliefs.

Frances Hook, who served with the 90th Illinois Infantry, was one of several women who enlisted, disguised as a man. Serving under the alias of Frank Fuller, she was captured at the Battle of Chattanooga. It was also in Chattanooga that the Confederates captured still another prize, Dr. Mary Elizabeth Walker, a contract surgeon with the Union Army.

During the Civil War, nurses were rather disliked by many doctors and often viewed as plain nuisances. Some 6,000 women served as nurses. Miss Dorothea Linde Dix, the internationally famous reformer of mental institutions and authoress of children's books, established the Union's Nurse Corps. Miss Dix's nurse corps was not an official part of the Union Army. The nurses were civilians who received twelve dollars a month as their salary, one ration a day, and their lodging. They were the lowest paid of anyone on the Army payroll.

Among the qualifications for a nurse in the Union Army was that she should not be young and beautiful, had to be over thirty years of age, and was required to wear either a brown or black dress. No hoop skirts, then in fashion, were allowed.

Another Civil War heroine was Annie Etheridge, a seventeen-year-old nurse who served with the 2nd Michigan Infantry. Though often referred to as "Gentle Annie," she participated in twenty-eight battles and had two horses killed beneath her. She received the Kearny Cross of Valor, one of the Union's highest decorations, for her heroism.

Service with naval forces also took place in the Civil War. The confiscated Confederate steamer, the *Red Rover,* became a Union Army hospital. Four nuns of the Order of the Holy Cross volunteered their services and became the first female nurses carried aboard a U.S. Navy hospital ship.

U.S. Signal Corps photos: Left: Belle Starr. Center: Dr. Mary Elizabeth Walker. Right: Clara Barton.

The sisters nursed patients on the *Red Rover* until its retirement on November 17, 1865.

Nurses also served aboard steamboats on both the Ohio and Mississippi rivers. These Civil War sternwheelers were the forerunners of the modern-day hospital ships that operated off the coasts of Korea, and more recently, the Republic of Vietnam in those wars where American fighting men again needed medical attention.

The War Between the States also brought Clara Barton to national prominence. After the end of the war she searched for, identified and marked over 12,000 graves of soldiers in Andersonville, Georgia. She was formerly a schoolteacher and government clerk. In 1881 she founded and became the first president of the American Red Cross. This humanitarian agency has been with our men on the battlefields in every war since its founding. The Red Cross is said to have started in 1861 when Clara Barton and other Union ladies nursed the wounded after the Union

Army, in its first battle with the Confederates, suffered a crushing and humiliating defeat at Bull Run, Virginia, some twenty-five miles from Washington.

After the Civil War, as settlers pushed steadily westward, many forts were established to protect them against Indian attack. Officers' wives frequently served as nurses for their husbands' regiments, while the enlisted men's wives served as laundresses. The enlisted men's row of quarters thus came to be known as "Soapsuds Row." Historic homesites of the Indian War period were inside the various frontier Army forts. Some of these are still in use, such as Fort Bliss, Texas.

This nomadic existence of the late 1800's was not a very glamorous or inviting life. At times of Indian uprisings it often became harrowing. Some of these women paid with their lives, for there were frequent casualties among them during that period. However, this unique type of woman was dedicated to being with her husband and sharing his life on the frontiers.

One such wife was Mollie McIntosh, whose husband was a lieutenant with General George C. Custer's ill-fated 7th Cavalry. She felt such pride in her husband's unit that she habitually wore the military cap.

During the Spanish-American War, nurses were again hired under civilian contract and served in the Philippines, Cuba, Puerto Rico, aboard troop ships, and in the United States. Although Florence Nightingale is credited with setting up the first British Nurse Corps during the Crimean War, she was not the first to think of the idea. Nine years before her birth, a U.S. Navy surgeon, Dr. William Paul Crillon Barton, advocated female nurses in the U.S. Navy. He went so far as to make this recommendation to the Secretary of the Navy in 1811.

As a result of the nurses' performance during the Spanish-American War, Congress established the Army Nurse Corps in 1901, and the Navy Nurse Corps in 1908.

Spanish-American War Nurses. *Armed Forces Institute of Pathology photograph.*

Although the approximately 21,500 nurses who served during World War I were an essential part of the Army and Navy, they did not have military rank, officer status, equal pay, or any of the present benefits. In 1944, partial equality in regard to military rank, pay, and benefits was finally granted.

In World War I the British established service organizations, called auxiliaries, especially for women. The women in these auxiliaries performed a number of non-combat duties. For the first time the demands of war made it vital that women be utilized for something besides nursing and clerical tasks. They were introduced to many new fields, such as military intelligence, law, and personnel.

When the United States declared war on Germany in April, 1917, it began training a huge Army to fight in France. General John J. Pershing, Commander-in-Chief of the American Expeditionary Forces in France, saw the contributions being made by the British auxiliaries. He

Marine Corps women reservists, at work on a brick wall in New York City, to help encourage enlistments, 1918. *Defense Dept. Photo (Marine Corps).*

became enthused and recognized this new source of military manpower as a solution to a problem that was slowing the war effort. His headquarters needed French-speaking telephone operators, and he suggested in October that qualified women be enlisted in the U.S. Army for that purpose. Back in Washington, however, they were not easily convinced, but the War Department compromised. The Army provided Pershing with a token force of female telephone operators, but they were hired under government contract as civilian employees since it was thought that the enlistment of women in the Army would not be legal.

General Pershing's unsuccessful attempt to enlist women gave the Navy an idea. They too could utilize women in administrative and other related types of work. The Navy solved its problem by finding a loophole in an existing law that stated that the Navy was authorized to accept the service of "persons." Since the sex of said persons was not specified, on August 12, 1918, Secretary of the Navy Josephus Daniels approved the acceptance of women in the U.S. Navy and Marine Corps.

This was the first time in the nation's history that women were not only permitted to enlist in the armed forces, but it also marked the first time they were allowed to wear a uniform.

The Navy signed up several thousand female volunteers as Yeomen, who were referred to as "Yeomanettes." The Marine Corps followed suit and enrolled several hundred women, who were called "Marinettes." Their slogan was "Free a Marine to Fight." Over 10,000 women in both the Navy and the Marine Corps served primarily in clerical positions to free men for combat duty. On July 30, 1919, the Yeomanettes and Marinettes were disbanded and once again the armed forces were strictly all-male organizations. But the value of women had been proven and it was a fact that would not be forgotten.

During the period between World War I and II, several studies were made regarding the efficient utilization of women during a wartime situation. Suggestions for using women in peacetime were turned down, mainly due to lack of interest, but also because the Army and Navy were reduced to a very small size and there were more men volunteers than spaces available. This situation changed with the start of World War II.

In 1942, Congresswoman Edith Nourse Rogers of Massachusetts crusaded for military service for women. Congress passed legislation in May that established the Women's Army Auxiliary Corps (WAAC). The bill was entitled, "A Bill to Establish a Women's Army Auxiliary Corps for Service with the Army of the United States."

Within three days after the passage of the bill, President Franklin D. Roosevelt signed it and swore in Oveta Culp Hobby, a Texas newspaper publisher, as the WAAC's first director with the rank of colonel.

The initial WAAC strength was 25,000; however, during

World War II more than 150,000 WAACs served in the United States, Europe, Africa, Alaska, Southwest Pacific, China, India and Hawaii.

In July, 1943, the WAAC had done so well that it was no longer an auxiliary and became a component of the Army. It was renamed the Women's Army Corps (WAC) in September. However, this new status was only for the duration of the war plus six months. Without a legislative change this meant the Women's Army Corps would be disbanded at that time.

In July of 1942, the U.S. Navy Women's Reserve was authorized. Miss Mildred McAfee, who at the time was president of Wellesley College in Massachusetts, was commissioned a lieutenant commander (equivalent to a major in the Army), and became the first WAVE director. The initials WAVES, standing for "Women Accepted for Volunteer Emergency Service," are still retained today, even though it is not the correct terminology for women of the U.S. Navy. By 1945 there were approximately 86,000 WAVES in the service of their country. These WAVES released approximately 50,000 men for sea duty.

Ruth Cheney Streeter, a former welfare worker and aviation enthusiast, became the first director of the Women Marines on January 29, 1943, with the rank of colonel. The peak strength of Women Marines during World War II was slightly over 19,000, the approximate size of a Marine Corps division. By December 7, 1945, two-thirds of the distaff corps of the Marines was disbanded. However a small group was retained in the Marine Corps Headquarters, which was to prove fortunate, because at the outbreak of the Korean War, mobilization of Women Marines was accomplished easily with these experienced people already on active duty.

Over 40,000 WACs were utilized by the Army Air Forces in nearly all the non-combat jobs. The Flying Training Command also instituted the Women's Flying Training

Program to train women pilots to ferry aircraft and relieve men for the job of fighting. Under the direction of famous aviatrix, Miss Jacqueline Cochran, the first fifty women began their training at Howard Hughes Air Field, Houston, Texas, on November 15, 1941. As ferry pilots, they were assigned to the War Department in Civil Service status and received $250 a month to fly light liaison and training planes within the United States.

Mrs. Nancy Harkness Love, another well-known aviatrix, directed the first Women's Auxiliary Ferrying Squadron. American women had flown earlier for the British Air Transport Auxiliary before Pearl Harbor. The first five women pilots for the British were assigned to a ferry pool at White Waltham, England and freed badly needed pilots during the Battle of Britain, one of the great turning points in the war that stopped Hitler's plan to invade England.

During World War II the SPARS—Women of the Coast Guard—was organized. The SPARS reached a top strength of 10,000 enlisted women and 1,000 officers. They greatly relieved the administrative burden of Coast Guardsmen, who in war serve under the control of the Navy, although retaining their own uniforms and organization.

In the nearly four years of World War II some 57,000 Army and Navy nurses saw duty. They were all commissioned officers. The Japanese captured five Navy nurses on Guam when they invaded that island in December, 1941. They remained prisoners of war at Zentusji, Japan, until August, 1942, when they were repatriated. On January 6, 1942, eleven Army nurses were captured at Manila and imprisoned at Santo Thomas College on the outskirts of the city. They remained prisoners for over three years and were not liberated until 1945.

By the end of that war in which fifty-four American women in uniform gave their lives, there was great public pressure to demobilize the armed forces and "bring the troops home."

Once again the armed forces shrank in size, from a wartime high of 12,124,418 to a low of 1,582,000 in 1946. Career opportunities for women seemed to be gone again as at the end of World War I.

Fortunately, feminine ingenuity and determination won out, and a bill was signed on June 12, 1948, that authorized service for women in the regular armed forces. This bill, Public Law 625, passed by the 80th Congress and signed by President Harry S. Truman, authorized "the enlistment and appointment of women in the Regular Army, Navy, Air Force and Marine Corps."

Equality had finally arrived. All the services agreed in the recommendation that women should become a permanent part of the armed forces. After many years of effort, women had won almost full equality with their male counterparts. However, women were still not to be assigned to combat duties and there were still some benefit restrictions, but all the old taboos were rapidly disappearing.

During the Korean War the distaff corps once again took over certain areas to free men for combat. But Secretary of Defense General George C. Marshall considered the pace of recruiting much too slow and in September, 1951, he asked fifty women representatives of various professions to come to Washington for a conference in the Pentagon.

As a result of this conference a committee was formed, the Defense Advisory Committee on Women in the Service (DACOWITS), which is still in existence and has its headquarters in the Pentagon. It has been instrumental in the improvement of women's services in such areas as benefits, pay and promotion opportunities.

In Vietnam, as in the past three wars, women of the U.S. Armed Forces capably served their nation. Of the nearly 2 million military personnel who have helped the South Vietnamese in their struggle for freedom, only a small portion of this total were women, but regardless of numbers, women in uniform again have done a remarkable job.

For example, in March, 1965, two WACs, Major Kathleen I. Wilkes and M/Sgt. Betty Adams, assisted Major Tran Cam Huong in setting up the Vietnamese Women's Armed Forces Corps. A complete basic training camp was built just outside of Saigon. Within nine months eight refresher classes and five basic training classes had graduated. By 1969, all the services were providing female advisors to the Vietnamese Women's Armed Forces Corps.

Women have served at the headquarters of the U.S. Military Assistance Command Vietnam, in Saigon. American nurses representing all three services were at Chu Lai, Da Nang, Saigon, and with the State Department's AID Program in the countryside. They not only have taken care of the U.S. personnel, but also have taught the Vietnamese people how to care for themselves, Many South Vietnamese women have been trained by American nurses to serve their own people.

American nurses were aboard hospital ships and aboard the medical evacuation planes that have flown daily throughout the country. Soldiers, sailors, marines and airmen have received the best medical care in history and evacuation by air was credited with reducing the mortality rate of casualties to less than 1 percent, the lowest percentage in any war.

Of the over 3,500 military nurses who have served, by 1969 seven nurses had given their lives in the Republic of Vietnam, six in aircraft and helicopter crashes and one due to enemy rocket fire.

Today there are over 41,000 women serving in the armed forces. As proof of their value to the nation the Department of Defense in 1969 eliminated the strength ceiling for women in the armed forces. In doing so it opened wider the doors of opportunity to women who seek a lifetime career or a short career before the lifetime career of marriage.

CHAPTER 2

The Four Armed Forces

Before World War II, all of the armed forces of the United States—the Army, Navy, and Marine Corps —were under the War and Navy departments. After World War II another uniformed service was created—the Air Force—and a separate government department was established.

To gain further efficiency, in 1947 the Department of Defense was created and all of the armed forces were put under its control. The Secretary of Defense became a member of the President's cabinet. At the same time the old cabinet posts of Secretaries of War and Navy were abolished.

Today, the Department of Defense is often called the "world's largest business." That description is accurate because each year nearly half of every tax dollar is spent on national defense. The Defense budget has increased from $9,782,000,000 in 1948 to $77,539,000,000 in 1970. The manpower strength increased from 2,442,000 military and civilian employees in 1947 to 4,865,000 in 1969 because of the war in Vietnam. Its normal size is 3½ million military and 1 million civilian personnel. The size of the armed forces is determined by Congress, although the President is the Commander-in-Chief and recommends to Congress what the number of men and women and types of equipment the Army, Navy, Air Force, and Marine Corps should have to protect the nation.

The Defense Department has three main organizations, called departments. They are the Army, Navy (including the Marine Corps, and in time of war the Coast Guard), and the Air Force. The "home office" or headquarters is the Pentagon building which is located just across the Potomac River from the nation's capitol.

The Secretary of Defense is one of the most powerful men in the world because he controls, for the President, the nation's armed forces, which are the strongest in the world. His mission, as chief adviser to the President on defense matters, is the present and future security of the United States. He can be likened to a president of a giant business. He has a vice president (the Deputy Secretary), a Chief Scientist (the Director of Research and Engineering), and seven executive vice presidents (Assistant Secretaries). In addition, he has a legal adviser (Office of the General Counsel), and Special Assistants who work with the Atomic Energy Commission and the Congress.

The Joint Chiefs of Staff (which consists of the chiefs of staff of all the military services) and the Unified and Specified Commands, which control all the fighting forces from each of the services, also are under him.

The Joint Chiefs of Staff control the combat forces which are placed under special organizations by area or by use. The area commands are called Unified Commands. They are: the European, Pacific, Alaskan, Southern, and Atlantic. The Specified Commands, those which have a special function, are the North American Air Defense, the Military Airlift Command and the Strategic Air Command. All of these, except the Strategic Air Command, are composed of fighting units from the Army, Navy, Marine Corps, and Air Force. The Strategic Air Command is completely manned by Air Force men and women.

There are also various supporting organizations, called agencies, within the Department. They were formed in the interest of economy to handle matters common to the four services. The Defense Atomic Support Agency, in cooperation with the Atomic Energy Commission, manages, tests and stores nuclear weapons, such as bombs and warheads for missiles. The Defense Contract Auditing Agency oversees defense contracts with industry to be sure the Government is getting its money's worth. The Defense Communications Agency, which is sometimes called the telephone-telegraph company of the Department, is the overseer of all worldwide electronic communications. The Defense Intelligence Agency, the secret military information-gathering agency, is responsible for providing information on the armed forces of other nations.

The Defense Supply Agency, the largest buyer and distributor of supplies in the world, purchases everything from shoestrings for a pair of GI boots to billions of gallons of petroleum. This, the largest of the agencies, is staffed by over 57,000 people and operates eighteen distribution centers.

ARMY

The Army, created in 1775, had a peak strength of 20,000 during the Revolutionary War. In 1970 it had a manpower strength of over 1½ million. The Army has

17⅓ active divisions, two-thirds of which are stationed overseas, and several thousand smaller units. The headquarters of the Department of the Army is in the Pentagon. Before World War II the various offices of the old War Department were scattered over the Washington, D.C. area in seventeen different buildings. The Pentagon, built by the Army at the start of World War II and intended eventually to be used as a Veterans Hospital in the peace that would follow, was constructed originally to bring all its offices under one roof. It took 13,000 men, working twenty-four hours a day, to build this complex of eighty-three acres of offices. After World War II the Navy moved its headquarters there and the Air Force, already there, merely exchanged Army uniforms for new blue uniforms and stayed in the same offices.

The civilian head of the Army is the Secretary. A four-star general is the Chief of Staff. Both are appointed by the President and approved by the Senate. The same is true for the Navy and Air Force. There are four major commands: the Combat Development, the Materiel, the Continental and the Overseas Commands.

The Combat Development Command, located at Fort Belvoir, Virginia, just south of Washington, D.C., anticipates future Army needs, such as types of forces, materiel and their most effective use. With the use of special troop units it conducts war games, operations, experiments, and research. It is developing the Army of tomorrow.

The Army Materiel Command Headquarters, located in Arlington, Virginia, a few miles south of the Pentagon, tests, buys, stores and distributes Army equipment. Its laboratories are used for development, its arsenals throughout the nation for storage, and its proving grounds for testing. It is the research and development and supply agency of the Army.

The job of the Continental Army Command, which has its headquarters at historic Fort Monroe, Virginia, is to train and educate the soldier. This is done at sixteen training centers throughout the nation. It also conducts the Reserve Officer Training Course at colleges and high schools. Part of its far-flung educational network is the U.S. Military Academy at West Point, New York, which was the first military academy. It was established in 1802.

In addition, the Continental Army Command is responsible for the ground defense of the United States. To accomplish this, the Army divides the nation into six Army areas: the First, Fort Jay, New York; the Second, Fort George C. Meade, Maryland; Third, Fort McPherson, Georgia; Fourth, Fort Sam Houston, Texas; Fifth, Chicago, Illinois; Sixth, Presidio, San Francisco, California; and the Military District of Washington, Washington, D.C. The Army Air Defense Command, a part of the North American Air Defense Command at Colorado Springs, Colorado, assists in guarding against air attack with the NIKE ground-to-air missiles.

The four overseas commands are: the Pacific, European, Alaskan, and Southern Army Forces. The U.S. Army Pacific, at Fort Shafter, Hawaii, has units in Japan, Korea, Vietnam, Thailand, and Okinawa. The 8th U.S. Army, a part of this command, has helped to maintain the peace in Korea for over fifteen years. The U.S. Army, Europe, located at Heidelberg, Germany, has troop units in Germany and Italy. In addition, to its role in the ensuring of peace in Europe, it patrols the Berlin Wall. In wartime, its units become part of the North Atlantic Treaty Organization (NATO). The arctic forces of the U.S. Army, Alaska, which has its headquarters at Fort Richardson, Alaska, defend the United States from invasion by land from the north. The safety of the Panama Canal Zone is the responsibility of the U.S. Army Forces, Southern Command, located at Fort Amador, Canal Zone. This tropical environment provides tropical training for Army personnel.

Today's Army is not only men with rifles but has its own aircraft, helicopters, hovercraft and missiles. In addition to tanks and armored vehicles, it operates a fleet of ships and small vessels for river warfare, such as marsh buggies.

NAVY

The Continental Navy, established in 1775, had 53 men-of-war during the Revolutionary War. After the War, the Navy was disbanded and all the ships were sold. Pirates, however, became too much of a problem for the nation's small Revenue Cutter Service and the *United States,* a warship launched in 1797, became the first major ship in the rebirth of the Navy.

The Navy Department was officially established in 1798, while the nation was fighting an undeclared war with France. By 1799 the Navy had grown to 49 ships. The needs of the Civil War led to the building of one of the world's most powerful navies—670 ships and 57,000 men.

At the end of World War II the United States Navy was the most powerful in the world. But due to demobilization, by 1947 the Navy had shrunk in size to 498,000 naval personnel and 356,000 civilian employees. In 1970 its size was 770,000 naval personnel and over 430,000 civilian employees. There are over 800 ships in the active fleet and hundreds in the mothball fleet, that is, in storage.

The Navy, like the other uniformed services, has a civilian in charge and a military leader who reports to him—the Secretary of the Navy and the Chief of Naval Operations. The Marine Corps Commandant is also responsible to the Secretary of the Navy and works in cooperation with the Chief of Naval Operations on common matters.

The Navy Department includes naval operating forces at sea as well as shore bases, but even has air bases far from the ocean, and naval bases on the Great Lakes.

The Navy has both fighting and service ships. The principal fighting ships are: the aircraft carriers, cruisers, submarines and destroyers. Some of the Navy's heavy cruisers carry 8-inch guns, which can drop shells on a target seventeen miles away. There are 41 Polaris submarines capable of launching intercontinental ballistic missiles while submerged. The Navy has over 8,500 aircraft, of which the majority operate off 15 attack aircraft carriers, which are the main offensive ships in the Atlantic and Pacific Fleets.

The service ships are: ammunition, hospital, mine layers, mine sweepers, oilers, repair ships, and tugs. Although the Navy is considered a force afloat, it is supported by large government shipyards, supply bases, naval bases—where the ships dock—plus air and training stations.

There are five Sea Frontiers, which are divisions of the three United States coasts and other geographical areas. These Frontiers are: Alaskan, Eastern, Caribbean, Hawaiian, and Western. The Sea Commands are: the Atlantic Fleet, based at Norfolk, Virginia, and the Pacific Fleet, based at Pearl Harbor, Hawaii. The 6th Fleet, which stays in the Mediterranean Sea, is part of the Atlantic Fleet. The 7th Fleet, which fought in Vietnam, is part of the Pacific Fleet. The United States is divided into fourteen Naval Districts from the United States to Pearl Harbor.

The Naval Materiel Command, located in Washington, D.C., in the old World War I Navy Building on Constitution Avenue near the White House, is the Navy's developer, buyer and builder. It is responsible for procuring ships, aircraft, and other equipment for the fleets, for purchasing supplies and developing new equipment and ships of the future naval forces. In addition, it operates laboratories and test centers.

The Navy governs nearly one hundred mandated islands in the Pacific Ocean, and like the other services, provides naval attachés and missions to foreign countries.

MARINE CORPS

On November 10, 1775, the Continental Congress called for the establishment of two Marine Corps battalions. After the war the Marines were disbanded, but Congress reestablished them as a separate service in 1798. Throughout the years the Marines have made more than three hundred landings on foreign shores, and thus have become known as "soldiers of the sea." They have traditionally been the first to fight and are referred to as "leathernecks" because of the leather neck bands they once wore. In 1947 the Marines were 93,000 strong. There were over 315,000 Marines in 1970 because of the Vietnam War.

The Marine Corps has its headquarters in Arlington, Virginia, not far from the Pentagon. The Commandant, appointed by the President, serves a four-year term. He sits as a member of the Joint Chiefs of Staff, but only deliberates on those matters pertaining to the Marine Corps.

The Marine forces ashore and afloat are those that are assigned to the Atlantic and Pacific Fleets. These forces consist of three divisions with three wings of aircraft and supporting units.

More than one-half of the Marines are assigned duty with the fleets on amphibious assault ships. Marines are also assigned to other warships. They have various duties aboard ship, such as guards, orderlies and gunners. Some Marine helicopter and aircraft squadrons are aboard carriers.

The Marine Security Forces are those Marines whose responsibility it is to guard our embassies, legations and consulates.

The Marines have their own officer and basic training centers, which are separate from the Navy, but the Navy provides the other support such as medical care, chaplains and schools.

In addition to basic infantry weapons such as rifles, machine guns and mortars, the Marines have tanks, aircraft, and helicopters. Marine pilots are trained by the Navy and fly the same type of aircraft as their counterparts in the Navy. The equipment for the Marine infantryman is often identical to that of the Army, which develops and tests most ground equipment for the Marine Corps.

AIR FORCE

During the Civil War the Union Army hired Thaddeus Lowe to observe Confederate movements from balloons. This method of aerial observation was next used during the Spanish War. Then, five years after they flew their flimsy biplane at Kill Devil Hill, North Carolina, the Wright Brothers sold the first military aircraft to the U.S. Army for $30,000. This began the uninterrupted history of what is known today as the United States Air Force. Until after World War II, land-based air power was a part of the Army and called the Air Corps. It gained independent status in 1947. In 1970 the Air Force had over 14,000 aircraft and 900,000 men and women in blue uniforms. It also has 1,054 intercontinental ballistic missiles in underground silos in the United States.

Along with its two sister services, the Air Force is organized under a civilian Secretary and a military Chief of Staff. Its headquarters is located in the Pentagon. The Air Force is divided into four general organizations: the Combat Commands, the Support Commands, the Training Commands and the Overseas Commands.

There are three fighting commands, the largest being the Strategic Air Command, which operates the nation's long-range bombers and land-based intercontinental ballistic missiles. Its headquarters is at Offut Air Force Base, Omaha, Nebraska. The pilots of this command fly the most sophisticated strategic bombers in the world while its missilemen maintain a vigil hundreds of feet below ground on a twenty-four-hour basis. The Tactical Air Command, Langley Air Force Base, Virginia, provides close air support for ground forces with fighter-bomber jet aircraft and it airlifts Army units in giant transports. The Air Defense Command, Ent Air Force Base, Colorado, is the nation's air defense force. Its supersonic jets are capable of reacting on a split second notice to intercept enemy bombers.

There are three major Air Force support commands: the Air Force Logistics Command, which is the supply agency; the Air Force Systems Command, which develops equipment for the Air Force of tomorrow, and the Military Airlift Command, which transports men and materials for all of the armed forces.

There are two training commands, the largest being the Air Training Command, which trains all Air Force personnel when they come into the service, and the Continental Air Command, which trains reserve personnel and the Air National Guard.

There are four major Air Force Commands overseas: the Air Forces in Europe, the Caribbean Air Command, the Alaskan Air Command, and the Pacific Air Forces.

COAST GUARD

The Coast Guard, dating back to 1790, was the only U.S. naval force after the Revolutionary War until the establishment of the regular U.S. Navy in 1798. As the Revenue Cutter Service, its original mission was the elimination of smuggling and piracy. In 1871 the additional job of assisting ships in distress was added. These two services, the Revenue Cutter and Lifesaving, were combined to form the U.S. Coast Guard in 1915. The responsibility to the nation is unchanged today, but is conducted on a much larger scale. Aircraft and helicopters have been added so that the Coast Guard can carry out its mission. When called upon, the Coast Guard has joined the naval forces in every war beginning with the undeclared war with France in 1798 through the war in Vietnam. In time of war, or when ordered by the President, the Coast Guard comes under the operational control of the Navy. In the Vietnam War, the Coast Guard cutters patrolled the South China Sea to prevent enemy infiltration by sea from the north.

During peacetime the Coast Guard is part of the Department of Transportation. Its organization is similar to that of the Navy and this facilitates easier mobilization and absorption into the Navy Department in wartime. Even the rank, customs, and traditions are alike. The Commandant of the Coast Guard has his headquarters in Washington, D.C., in the Department of Transportation Building.

The Coast Guard maintains an academy at New London, Connecticut. With the exception of recruit basic training, the majority of its training is done at U.S. Navy facilities.

There are over 30,000 Coast Guardsmen on active duty and over 32,000 reservists. Throughout the United States the Guardsmen man over 300 port security and 50 shipping inspection offices, over 500 patrol and lookout stations, and more than 500 lighthouses. In addition, the Coast Guard has several hundred vessels, including cutters, icebreakers, lifeboats, motorboats, surfboats, tenders, tugs and fire boats. Approximately 200 of these vessels are armed with machine guns, and some larger ships are armed with 5-inch guns. In addition, the Guard has special aircraft, including helicopters which are used for patrol and rescue operations.

It has only been within the past fifty years that these proud services have allowed women to serve in their uniformed ranks. Only in the last thirty years have they begun to accept them as equals, and only since 1948 have they been legally a part of the regular establishment.

CHAPTER 3

Ladies in Uniform

In 1948 women battered down one of the last remaining male bastions—the regular military and naval forces. In less than twenty years they reached the point where it was possible for a woman to command a school or base, even to be promoted to the rank of general. By 1969 women in uniform were recognized for their ability and not penalized for their sex.

Today, approximately 41,000 uniformed ladies of the armed forces are stationed throughout the world. In 1969 approval was granted to lift previous restrictions on their numbers. They hold jobs of every conceivable nature. A woman might be a secretary in an office in Washington, an air controller working in an airport tower in California, an aerospace nurse for the astronauts at Cape Kennedy or working in public relations in New York City. Women, whatever their job, play a vital part in the defense of the nation and their value to each of their own services has been proven many times. They do not just replace men, they compete equally with them for jobs and promotions. Nowhere in American society do women really have more equal job opportunities than in the military services.

There are ten components that make up the Defense Department's distaff corps: the Women's Army Corps (WAC), the Navy's WAVES, Women Marines, the Women in the Air Force (WAF), the Army Nurse Corps, Army Women's Medical Specialist Corps, the Navy Nurse Corps, Navy Medical Service Corps, Air Force Nurse Corps, and the Air Force Women's Medical Specialist Corps. There are also the Coast Guard's SPARS.

THE WACS

The Women's Army Corps (WAC), which is head-quartered in the Pentagon in Washington, D.C. is the oldest female component authorized by Congress. Its history began in 1942 with the formation of the Women's Army Auxiliary Corps (WAAC). During World War II some 17,000 women served overseas in the WAACs. In 1970 there were over 13,000 WACs on duty with the Army, of which some 12,000 were enlisted and 1,000 commissioned officers.

The director of the WAC is a colonel and she reports directly to the Secretary of the Army and to the Chief of Staff.

WACs serve on Army installations in every corner of the globe—Germany, Greece, Italy, Belgium, Hawaii, Japan, Korea, Okinawa, Vietnam, Thailand, and Taiwan.

The original mission of the WAC was to relieve men for combat duties. They still may serve only in jobs not directly related to combat, or unbecoming to a woman. The WACs in World War II not only proved their capability to free men for combat, but proved also that women could do many jobs as well or better than men. Women at first served in the fields of either administration, medicine, communications, personnel, intelligence or public information, but few career fields are now closed. WACs today are eligible for duty in 165 of the Army's 469 career fields, which include air defense radar operators, finance, recruiting, special services, data processing, court reporter, and medical technicians.

WACs are trained at historic Fort McClellan, near Anniston, Alabama. Training for newly enlisted women lasts for eight weeks. Upon graduation they are sent to specialized schools for further education and technical training.

Commissioned officer training lasts for eighteen weeks and is conducted only twice a year. The tour of duty for an officer with the Army is a minimum of two years. The enlisted tour is anywhere from three to six years, depending upon the type of enlistment.

ARMY NURSE CORPS AND ARMY WOMEN'S MEDICAL SPECIALIST CORPS

The Army Nurse Corps built commendable rcords during World Wars I and II. During World War I, 21,500 nurses were in uniform. In World War II there were 57,000 nurses on duty. Of this group 16 were killed, 63 were taken prisoners and over 1,600 were decorated for bravery.

After being commissioned as officers, Army nurses attend an eight-week orientation course at the Brooks Army Medical Center located at Fort Sam Houston, Texas, which is a part of greater San Antonio. There are presently over 5,000 Army nurses of which 4,000 are women. Army nurses or specialists may have a variety of assignments, such as staff members of hospitals around the world, as teachers, supervisors in the Office of the Surgeon General in Washington, D.C., or on special projects such as advising military nurses of friendly nations.

WAVES

The Navy was the most farsighted of all the services when it came to recognizing the value of women in the military. The Navy and Marine Corps first enlisted women in 1918 after discovering a loophole in Navy regulations. After one year of service during World War I, the 10,000 women who had served as Yeomanettes and Marinettes were disbanded.

In 1942, the Navy again recruited women and during World War II some 86,000 women served as WAVES. Most of them were released from active duty at the end of the war, but the Navy kept a small number of WAVES on active duty. Then in 1948, with the passage of the Women's Armed Services Integration Act, the Navy joined with the other services and recruited women.

The WAVES have their headquarters in Arlington Annex, adjacent to the Pentagon, overlooking Arlington Cemetery. From her office, in Arlington, Virginia, the director, a Navy captain, oversees the recruiting, training and assignment of the WAVES. They are assigned to the same career fields as men, but cannot serve on combat ships. There are usually some 6,000 enlisted WAVES and approximately 600 officers on active duty. Since 1945, WAVES have been assigned overseas.

WAVES receive their basic training at the Recruit Training Command, Bainbridge, Maryland, on the shores of the Susquehanna River. After an intensive ten-week course, over 70 percent of all recruits go to specialized schools. The remainder go to jobs they are qualified for because of previous education or experience. Some of the twenty fields available to enlisted WAVES are: journalist, date processing, radioman, air controlman, administration, medicine, or photographer's mate.

Officer candidates are trained at the U.S. Naval Women Officers School, Newport, Rhode Island. After completion of a sixteen-week course there are over twenty fields the lady officer may be assigned to for her first job. Some of these are: international relations, intelligence, oceanography, public relations, education, or as a liaison officer on Capitol Hill working to provide information requested by senators and congressmen.

WAVES are allowed to serve aboard ships such as hospital ships and naval transports. They frequently are assigned to Navy shore stations around the world, such as Italy, Japan, England, Spain, or Hawaii.

NAVY NURSE CORPS AND MEDICAL CORPS

The Navy Nurse Corps and Navy Medical Corps are unique because they serve both Navy and Marine Corps personnel and their families. Every speciality in nursing is found in the Navy Nurse Corps; such as nuclear nursing, anesthesia, research and clinical areas.

The minimum tour of duty for this all-commissioned officer corps is two years. There is no special orientation for the nurses or medical specialists. They need only attend the training school in Newport, Rhode Island, for the indoctrination course for new officers. Nurses may be assigned to hospitals either in the United States or in foreign countries, aboard Military Sea Transport Ships, or aboard one of the Navy's hospital ships, such as the U.S.S. *Sanctuary* or U.S.S. *Repose*. There are at present over 2,200 nurses on duty with the Navy.

WAF

The Women in the Air Force (WAF) belong to the aerospace team. They are part of the youngest of the military services but their traditions are carried on from the Women's Army Corps of World War II.

Known as Air WACs, more than 40,000 served with the Army Air Forces during World War II. At the end of that war, when women in the Army were being demobilized, 1,500 were transferred into the Air Force in 1947 to become the first WAF. It was not until 1948 that women were recognized as part of the regular Air Force.

The Director of the WAF, wearing the eagle insignia of a colonel, has her office in an outer office of the Pentagon that overlooks the Potomac River. She and her staff are part of the staff of the Office of the Deputy Chief of Staff for Personnel.

In 1970 there were over 14,000 women in the Air Force. In the WAF, approximately 1,000 are officers and 8,500 are enlisted. There are also 3,800 nurses and 220 medical specialists who are commissioned officers.

Officer and basic training are both conducted at Lackland Air Force Base, Texas, which is next to historic Kelly Field and near the city of San Antonio. The officers are trained in coeducational classes along with their male counterparts.

After basic training enlisted women attend specialized training courses that can last anywhere from four to twenty-two weeks in length. Courses of instruction are conducted at various bases throughout the United States. Some WAF, because of their previous experience and education, are sent directly to their first job.

WAF serve in all career fields in the Air Force other than as a member of a combat aircrew or any job directly related to combat, such as the arming of nuclear weapons. There are no "strictly WAF jobs," other than as commanders of

WAF squadrons or units, and the job of the Director of the WAF. Women are in competition with men for various assignments in the Air Force and are trained and promoted under the same policies and procedures.

Enlisted WAF find themselves working in intelligence, weather, communications, personnel, medical, accounting, photo-mapping, and public information career fields. The fields for officers include science, engineering, space analyst, biological chemist, public information, weather physicist, ground electronics officer, television, education, and intelligence.

WAF are stationed around the world. They are in Hawaii, Japan, Turkey, England, Alaska, Germany, Italy, and Greece. One fourth of the WAF are stationed at bases in foreign countries.

AIR FORCE MEDICAL SERVICE

In 1949 the Air Force Medical Service was established. This service includes the doctors, dentists, veterinarians, nurses, dieticians, and physical and occupational therapists. Air Force medical personnel do primarily the same job for the Air Force as their civilian counterparts perform in their communities. They are responsible not only for the health of Air Force personnel, but for their dependents as well.

The newly commissioned second lieutenant, after six weeks of specialized training, may become an air-evac nurse, a nursing field peculiar only to the Air Force Nurse Corps. Or after one year of additional training she may become an aerospace nurse and work with the astronauts at Cape Kennedy.

Nurses and women of the Biomedical Science Corps, all of whom are officers, are assigned to dispensaries and hospitals around the world. The first assignment is usually at a hospital in the United States. The minimum tour is for two years.

MARINES

Women have been serving in the Marine Corps for over twenty-seven years. Since 1943, more than 40,000 women have worn Marine Corps uniforms. The Marine Corps Women's Reserve reached an all-time high of over 19,000 in World War II. Most of these women were discharged after the war, although a small number remained on duty. A year and a half after the signing of the act which established the distaff corps, the Marine Corps Women's Reserve reached its goal of 18,000 enlisted and 1,000 officers. At present there are nearly 3,000 women Marines on active duty across the world. Of this number, approximately 300 are officers and the remainder are enlisted.

Basic training for women Marines is conducted at the Marine Corps Recruit Depot, Parris Island, South Carolina, which is also the East Coast training center for male Marines. It is located near Beaufort, South Carolina. The training lasts for seven weeks. Most basic trainees go on to a specialized school. The few who are qualified are assigned to jobs immediately upon graduation. The required enlistment is three or four years.

Women Marines are hardly limited in their choice of fields. The only restricted category is duty with a combat ship or aircraft. In addition, they may not serve with the Fleet Marine Force. The variety of jobs include photography, aviation operations, intelligence, personnel, and communications.

For many years women Marines were not permitted to be stationed overseas. However, the restrictions were lifted in 1949 and Women Marines, both officer and enlisted, are now assigned to Vietnam, Japan, Okinawa, Italy, Germany, England, Belgium, Lebanon, the Panama Canal Zone, and the Philippines.

The Women's Officer Candidate Course is the first step in the building of a female Marine Corps officer. This course takes nine weeks and is conducted twice a year at the Marine Corps School, Quantico, Virginia, which is some thirty miles south of Washington, D.C. With the exception of male officers obtained from the service academies, all Marine officers are trained here. After completion of the Officer Candidate Course, she attends a seven-week basic course. She may then go on to one of several schools in her field of capability. The minimum tour of duty for an officer is three years.

The Director of the Women Marines is a colonel. Her office, in the headquarters of the Marine Corps, is in the Arlington Annex Building, adjacent to the Pentagon.

SPARS

The Coast Guard Women's Reserve (SPARS) derived its name from *Semper paratus* ("Always Ready"), the Coast Guard motto. Created on November 23, 1942, it was the smallest women's service in World War II. By August, 1945, some 10,000 enlisted women and 1,000 women officers were serving in the Coast Guard.

They were originally trained at Palm Beach, Florida, and Manhattan Beach, New York. After the war the officers were released to inactive duty and the enlisted women were discharged.

The headquarters of the SPARS is located in the Department of Transportation building in Washington, D.C. There are less than a dozen officers on active duty. They serve only on the headquarters staff during peacetime. In time of war they would also become part of the Department of the Navy. During peacetime there are no enlisted women on active duty, and at the present neither officers nor enlisted women are being accepted for training.

If accepted, enlisted women in the Coast Guard would be trained with the Navy's WAVES at Bainbridge, Maryland. There are several organized Reserve Training Units across the United States which accept applicants. A few are accepted for active service as officers for Coast Guard duty if they have prior military service.

Coast Guard women serve in a variety of fields, such as finance, communications, intelligence, personnel, and as hospital corpsmen. In time of war they would be called upon to relieve Coast Guardsmen for more dangerous duties.

How does one get into one of these organizations, whether for a career or for a period of time to serve their nation while learning a skill?

CHAPTER 4

Decision Time

In this, the last third of the twentieth century, a woman can expect to live to be at least seventy-four years old. Women already outnumber men three to one and by 1980 over 36 million women will be a part of our working society. These statistics from the Women's Bureau of the Department of Labor show a definite trend in the role of women today, and their importance to the future. More women will have careers other than in the home and for many women a career may be a necessity. Whether a woman plans either marriage or a career in the commercial world, training in some job field will mean not only present security but a life insurance policy for her later years. Each year the cost of schooling rises and for many girls the training offered by the armed forces will be the only way to learn a skill. Surely some will select uniformed life as a career.

THE FIRST STEP

Each year many girls consider entering the armed forces after graduation from high school or college. For some it is for the further education and training they cannot afford, for some it is adventure and new places, for others it is answering a call to serve their nation. For all, the path is pretty much the same.

Usually, information about career opportunities in each of the armed forces is obtained by going to the local recruiting office or to a nearby military installation or naval base. If neither is convenient, she may write to one of the following addresses:

ARMY
Commanding General
U.S. Army Recruiting Command
Liberty Building, 1520 Aberdeen Road
Hampton, Virginia 23364

NAVY
Bureau of Naval Personnel (Pers B622)
Department of the Navy
Washington, D.C. 20370

MARINE CORPS
Commandant of the Marine Corps (Code DP)
Headquarters, U.S. Marine Corps
Washington, D.C. 20380

AIR FORCE
Headquarters, USAF Recruiting Service
Randolph AFB, Texas 78148

ENLISTING

A girl, upon taking her oath as a recruit, receives $124.50 a month during her basic training. This is over and above her first uniforms, which are provided, and other cash allowances. The enlisted pay range goes all the way up to $903.60 a month for a sergeant major with over twenty-six years of service, or $1,054.50 a month for a Chief Warrant Officer with over twenty-six years of service.

From the very moment she takes her oath she starts to receive thirty days paid vacation each year, complete medical and dental care, and an excellent insurance program. In addition, social security deductions are made from her salary and she begins building benefits in that program. How long is her enlistment? The minimum enlistment in the Army is three years, in the Navy three years, in the Marine Corps three years, and in the Air Force four years. If the enlistee should decide to return to civilian life at the end of her enlistment she is entitled to the same veterans' benefits men receive, such as assistance in paying for college tuition and low-cost GI Bill home loans. The armed forces even help find jobs for those who do not reenlist.

The qualifications for enlistment in each of the services vary only in age requirements. Basically, they all require that the young lady be an American citizen (or have declared her intent to become one), be unmarried at the time of enlistment, have no dependents under eighteen years of age, and have a high school diploma or the equivalent, which is determined by making a passing score on a General Educational Development Test if not a graduate.

The two most important requirements are that one must be in good physical health and be of excellent moral character. The minimum age for enlistment is eighteen. None of the services will accept a girl under twenty-one years of age without the written consent of her parents or guardian. The Army will accept women up through thirty-four years of age, the Navy to twenty-five years of age, the Marine Corps to twenty-nine years of age, and the Air Force to twenty-seven.

A future WAC taking a test prior to enlistment. *U.S. Army photo.*

THE NEXT STEP

Having decided to enlist, the next step is to go to a recruiting office of the service chosen. Here is generally what she will experience, regardless of whether she wants to be a WAC, WAVE, WAF or Marine. After chatting with her to determine that she meets the basic requirements, the recruiter will give her a fifteen-minute screening test. If she passes this initial mental exam she will fill out an application for enlistment. The recruiter will then schedule her for a future appointment. This appointment will take an entire day and will consist of testing, a complete medical examination, additional interviews, and the filling out of more forms. If this testing is to be done outside of her community, and she has no means of transportation, the recruiter will make transportation arrangements. On this day of pre-enlistment testing, to stay one step ahead of the game, she should bring her parents' written consent, if she is under twenty-one, and her birth certificate, and high school diploma or General Educational Development Test results. GED tests can be arranged through your local high school guidance office.

After the medical examination, which is given by a military doctor and nurse team, she will be given mental tests. These tests not only determine her mental capabilities, but they are also aptitude tests designed to reveal the job areas she is most suited for. The armed forces make every attempt to put their people in jobs they like and will do well at. After these tests are completed the girl will be interviewed and asked to fill out additional forms. These forms are very similar to those of job application forms used by civilian businesses. She will be asked for personal references, references from previous employers and schools. She will have to complete a Statement of Law Violations and there will be a routine police check. If she has been in a mental hospital a report will be required from that hospital. She will fill out an emergency data form on which she will give names, addresses and telephone numbers of next-of-kin to be notified in case of an emergency.

A personal history form, on which she lists every place she has ever lived since birth, must be filled out. Even if during her lifetime she only moved a block away, this must be included. This information will be used by the FBI to investigate and verify the enlistee's background before she will be permitted to have access to or work with classified information. In addition, she will fill out an Armed Forces Security Questionnaire on which she will be asked to answer questions such as: "Have you ever belonged to the Communist Party?" This is to determine whether or not she has ever been involved in subversive activities.

Unless there is some unforeseen complication a girl is told the same day whether or not she will be accepted for service.

How long does she wait before leaving for basic training?

Enlistees are given a choice of enlistment dates. Whether she would like to report immediately or wait thirty to sixty days is up to her. If she wants to be sworn in that same day it is not impossible. However, most girls find they like to go home, tell everyone good-bye, and get their personal belongings before reporting for basic training.

On the date she and the service have agreed is most convenient, the enlistee will report back to the Armed Forces Entrance and Examining Station.

All reservations and tickets will be taken care of by the service recruiter. If the physical examination was more than ten days prior to the reporting date she will have to undergo a physical recheck. This is a review of records and a weight check. She will then be given the oath of enlistment, sign her enlistment papers and then she is on her way. From this moment on, even though she is still in civilian clothes, she is a part of the military and her pay has begun.

Having fulfilled the necessary requirements, the WAC applicant is sworn in and becomes a member of the United States Army. *U.S. Army photo.*

From the recruiting station she will either be flown, bussed, or sent by train to the basic training center.

Although she will now be referred to as private, seaman candidate, or airman, in this profession once exclusively for men, she is still a "Miss" and treated as a lady at all times.

OFFICER REQUIREMENTS

The qualifications for officer candidates differ slightly with each service. All the services require that the applicant be an American citizen—except the Army which will accept someone who has established permanent residency—have a baccalaureate degree, and meet the physical, mental and moral requirements. The Marine Corps will not accept an applicant with a degree in medicine, dentistry, veterinary medicine or theology, for duty in those fields because the Marine Corps relies on the Navy for those services.

As with enlistees the age requirements differ. The Army officer range is from 20 through 32, the Navy 20-27, the Marine Corps 21–29 and the Air Force 20½–29½. The Navy, Air Force, and Marine Corps will accept married officer candidate applicants, however the Army will not accept a married officer candidate. This marriage restriction is lifted after officer candidate training is completed.

NURSE REQUIREMENTS

With two exceptions, the requirements for the three services' Nurse Corps are the same as those for WAC, WAVE, WAF, and Marine Corps officers. First, the applicant must be currently registered as a professional nurse and must meet certain age limitations. The Army age requirement is that she be no older than 33, but applicant will be accepted up to age forty if she has had 7 years of prior military service. The Naval nurse age limitation is 34 and the Air Force is 35 years of age. Even though the requirements are strict there are service programs in which a girl enlists for nurse training and agrees to serve a specified amount of time after graduation as a nurse.

All the Medical Specialist Corps in the Army, Navy, and Air Force are officer corps. Therefore, their requirements are the same as those of the other officers, except that they must have a baccalaureate degree or internship in dietetics, physical therapy or occupational therapy. The age requirements also vary in these corps. The Army and Navy Medical Specialist Corps accept applicants from 20 to 32, and the Air Force from 21 to 35 years of age.

The steps involved in applying for an officer's commission are only slightly different from that of the normal enlistment.

A recruiting office, for example, will make an appointment with the selection representative of the service the college graduate is interested in. Depending on the section of the country it could either be a young lady fresh out of college who has completed her officer training, or a noncommissioned officer. The applicant should be prepared to give the selection officer a 3- by 5-inch head and shoulder photograph, a college transcript and a birth certificate. From this point forward she will fill out numerous forms, take a physical examination and complete a test to determine her fields of interest. A National Security Agency check into the applicant's background, conducted by the FBI, using information provided by the officer candidate, must be completed before she will be accepted. There will be a minimum waiting period of sixty to ninety days before the processing of the application is completed, but the applicant can expect to be notified of acceptance within thirty days.

The starting pay of a second lieutenant is $577.20 a

month. In addition, the officer receives monetary allowances for housing, food, and an initial clothing purchase grant. The pay scale, which is the same as for men, then ranges all the way to the rank of general at a salary of $2,750.40 a month after twenty-six years of continuous service. Additional service benefits include educational assistance, medical care and dental care, retirement and social security benefits.

Each of the services has programs for women currently enrolled in college. The Army offers college students a four-week indoctrination into service life with no obligation to join. This is conducted each summer at Fort McClellan, Alabama. The requirements are the same as that of an officer, except that applicants must have completed the junior year of college. Transportation to and from Fort McClellan is paid for by the Army. During this time the prospective officer candidate is paid a corporal's salary and is referred to as a cadet. She is issued uniforms, receives free medical and dental care, and meets other college juniors while receiving classroom instruction on the Army. Application for this program should be made before completing the junior year. Successful completion of this four-week course establishes eligibility for enrollment in the WAC Student Officer Program. Under this program a college senior may receive the pay and allowances of a corporal (approximately $438 monthly). Upon graduation she is commissioned as a second lieutenant with a two-year obligation.

The Navy offers an eight-week officer-candidate training course at Newport, R.I., to candidates between their junior and senior years. They are commissioned an ensign and sent back to Newport for an additional eight weeks of indoctrination before reporting to their first assignment. The Marine Corps also offers a college junior program.

The Air Force Reserve Officer Training Course is open to women in four different colleges: Auburn University,

Auburn, Alabama; Drake University, Des Moines, Iowa; East Carolina University, Greenville, North Carolina; and Ohio State University, Columbus, Ohio. Participants must meet all officer-candidate requirements and attend a six-week training course before their junior year. They then attend AFROTC classes during the junior and senior year and receive approximately $50 a month. Upon graduation they are commissioned a second lieutenant in the Air Force.

NURSES

There are several financial aid programs which enable women to become a nurse in the armed forces. Programs are for both high school graduates and girls already enrolled in a nursing school. For example, the Navy will finance the last two years of nurse or medical specialist training. This financing includes everything: tuition, books, living expenses, and pays the student $248 a month. Six months before graduation the student is commissioned an ensign and becomes a member of the Navy on a salary of $577.20 a month. For those who enroll in this program as juniors there is a requirement to serve three years, and two years if the program is started while a senior.

When she starts basic training or officer candidate training a girl will find that she has in store some exhausting weeks of strenuous and sometimes hilarious moments which mold her into a woman who has earned the right to wear the uniform of her country.

CHAPTER **5**

Training the Recruit

One thing every recruit has in common, no matter which of the four services she joins, is basic training. This period of time forms the basis for her career in the armed forces and her first introduction into an exciting and fascinating world. It is a new experience and for some girls will be the first time away from home. The armed forces realize this and try to take the recruit through this period with both firmness and understanding.

Each of the services maintain their individual basic training facilities. All of the training bases are located in the southern part of the United States.

The Army Basic Training Center is at Fort McClellan, which is near Anniston, Alabama. The Navy Basic Training Center is located at Bainbridge, Maryland, which is north of Baltimore. The Marine Corps Basic Training

WAC barracks for basic trainees at Fort McClellan, Alabama. *U.S. Army photo.*

Center is at Parris Island, South Carolina, and the Air Force Basic Training Center is at Lackland Air Force Base near San Antonio, Texas.

No matter which service she has chosen, the recruit can expect to be met upon arrival at the town nearest the basic training center. If by chance she is not met at the various bus, train and air terminals, there are signs posted with telephone numbers to call to get transportation to the center. The recruit is never stranded intentionally and all she needs do is to let someone know she has arrived.

Joining one of the armed forces does not mean a girl stops being feminine. In making plans for the trip the recruit should plan on taking the things she would generally take on a one-week trip. Each of the services gives the new enlistee a recommended list of things to bring and what to leave home for the period of basic training.

At the center she will be issued summer and winter

uniforms, shoes, purse, overcoat, etc.—complete ward-robes. A woman Marine receives an allowance and buys her own undergarments. However, to tide her over during the first week before she receives all these items, it is suggested she bring the following things: four changes of either nightgown or pajamas, robe, low-heeled shoes, four each of panties and bras and four pairs of nylons. Depending on the season, she should bring either a coat and sweater or a bathing suit. In addition, she will need a dress, slacks or shorts, and a blouse. This is for evening and off-duty wear.

She might also bring stationery, stamps, camera and, of course, cosmetics; however all of the things needed can be purchased at the center's exchange.

Because she will not have as much room at the center as she had at home, such things as bulky stereo sets, hair dryers and a television set should not be brought. Day rooms and recreation facilities have television sets. Hair dryers, irons and ironing boards are also available.

Within the first week, trainees get paid approximately $50. This varies with each service, but it is advisable to bring a minimum of $20 to last until this first pay day. However, if the recruit needs money, the needed purchases can be charged at the exchange store until she receives her first check. She will be paid every two weeks.

WACS

The Army conducts basic training for women in the foothills of the Appalachian Mountains at Fort McClellan, Alabama. The training course lasts for eight weeks. At the end of this highly concentrated training period the majority of the enlistees go to one of the Army's specialist schools to learn a skill such as typing, electronic repair, financial accounting, or control tower operation.

When she arrives in Anniston, whether it be by plane, bus or train, there will be a sign which reads: "Women's Army Corps Incoming Personnel call Fort McClellan for transportation." The telephone number to call is also posted on the sign.

When she arrives at her home for the next eight weeks she will be taken to the Headquarters and Receiving Company, which is the training battalion. She will be assigned to a platoon of approximately thirty-eight girls who live in a dormitory-type atmosphere.

After a brief introduction to the Army and what it expects out of its new members, the new WAC begins using

WAVE company from U.S. Naval Training Center, Bainbridge, Maryland, pass in review. *U.S. Navy photo.*

her Social Security number for identification on all Army records, such as a locator card. The locator card makes sure she receives her mail promptly and any telephone calls from home or friends. The first thing she will learn after being issued linens is how to make her bed in the military style and how to store her clothes into unbelievably small places. This is all part of the training and teaches the recruit discipline and how to take orders. One day she will be giving orders and the Army has learned from long experience that before giving orders one must learn to take them.

The uniform the new WAC is issued is dark green in color and is altered to fit the individual's figure. It consists of a two-piece suit of a wool blend with a beige cotton blouse. The summer uniform is made of a wash-and-wear material. It is also green but with white pin stripes. The green cap is similar to that worn by some airline stewardesses, and the shoes are black pumps.

Once again, the new WAC begins a round of tests which are designed to reveal her hidden abilities and interests in various fields. After the test results have been reviewed she will be interviewed by a counselor. This counselor is trained to determine the recruit's interests and abilities and relate them to a "Military Occupational Speciality (MOS)," the Army's way of saying "jobs in the military."

The processing takes nearly all of the first week of basic training. The remaining seven weeks are spent in classroom instruction, drilling, and learning how to get along with people.

The day begins at 6 A.M., with classes starting at 8 A.M. In these classes the recruit will learn military history and traditions, such as the story behind "the salute." She will be instructed in first aid and personal hygiene because the Army wants its girls to know the proper application of makeup, basic rules of fashion and simple etiquette.

Lights go out at 10 P.M. There are no weekend passes or overnight passes during the eight weeks of basic training.

A WAVE is instructed on extinguishing fire at Fleet Training Center, San Diego. *U.S. Navy photo.*

Some passes are given to girls after the second week to attend the post theater on Fort McClellan or a movie in nearby Anniston.

If she maintains an acceptable academic average, in addition to adjusting to the strict military life, the new WAC will graduate from basic training. If she does not, she is discharged and sent home. This applies to all of the armed forces.

Upon graduation she is given fourteen days of vacation before reporting to school or to her first assignment. The majority of girls attend one of the vocational speciality schools, such as Finance, Information, Intelligence, Chemical, Medical, Food Service, Signal, Adjutant General, Engineer Quartermaster, Medical and Administration. Some are assigned directly to jobs because they are already qualified. Others receive training on the job.

WAVES

The Navy Recruit Training Command for Women is at Bainbridge Naval Training Center, which is located on the Susquehanna River some thirty miles northeast of Baltimore. Upon arrival in Perryville, the nearest town, the new WAVE will call for transportation to the Naval Training Center.

The first week at Bainbridge is spent in processing. When she arrives at Bainbridge she will be taken in tow by company aides. The new recruits are formed into companies and assigned dormitory-type living quarters. A senior petty officer will be assigned as the company commander. During the ten weeks of training she will be in charge. She selects some promising recruits to serve as company petty officers. These girls assist her in administrative matters and other duties. This is the first exposure to leadership.

The Navy's WAVE uniform was created by the famed fashion designer, Mainbocher. The winter uniform is a two-piece suit of dark blue serge, worn with a white blouse and black tie. The hat is a smart blue and white. A pale blue and white pin-striped cotton suit with a matching hat is worn in the summer. For extra special occasions there is a dress white uniform.

The WAVE basic training day begins early, at 5:20 A.M. The WAVE recruit has until 6 A.M. to dress and make her bed. From 6 to 7:30 she has breakfast and then tidies up the barracks. From 7:30 to 8:15 is inspection time. Promptly at 8:30 A.M. classes begin. She attends eight classes of forty minutes' duration each, five days a week. There are three ten-minute breaks between classes. From 11:40 A.M. until 1:00 P.M. lunch is served and then it is back to class. During the hours from 4:00 to 9:00 P.M. the new WAVE has dinner and then time for personal things such as writing letters or just relaxing. She has from 9:00 until 9:25 P.M. to prepare for "lights out" at 9:30.

Beginning the second week, the new Navy enlistee may use the recreation facilities in Bainbridge, such as the gym, pool and the WAVE store. On the fifth weekend at Bainbridge members of the immediate family are invited to visit either Saturday or Sunday, but not on both days. When she enters her sixth week of basic the WAVE is given liberty to use the theater, the enlisted personnel club and the bowling alley. Also, either on the sixth or seventh weekend, she is

WACs march to class during basic training, Fort McClellan, Alabama. *U.S. Army photo.*

granted off-base leave for an afternoon or evening. On the eighth Saturday she is offered an optional guided tour of Washington, D.C.

Her training will consist of instructions on Navy history, ships, aircraft, customs and traditions. She will receive a charm and grooming course. In addition to normal classroom instruction, every WAVE must attend the swimming and physical training classes. In order to graduate from basic training the WAVE must be able to swim.

Trainees are tested weekly on the material covered. To complete basic training they must maintain an acceptable average.

One week of the basic training is spent in actual on-the-job experience. This could range from messenger to a cleaning detail. In the third week of training each girl is put on a list for security watch, which she will stand for two or three hours every third day. Also during the third week she will spend half a day taking Navy classification tests. She will also be interviewed regarding training for a speciality. But it depends on the Navy's needs and the WAVE's capabilities as to what school she will be assigned after basic training.

MARINES

The Marine Corps trains its distaff corps in the Deep South at the Marine Corps Recruit Depot, Parris Island, South Carolina. Marine Corps basic training lasts eight weeks.

When she arrives at Parris Island, the trainee is assigned to a forming platoon of approximately seventy girls. The first week is spent in fitting of uniforms, medical and dental examinations and other processing matters.

The Marine Corps uniform is designed by Mainbocher, who designed the WAVE uniform. It is a two-piece

"Marine Green" suit. The summer uniform is of a pin-striped wash-and-wear Dacron material. Both are extremely chic and altered to fit each girl.

The enlistee's day at boot camp begins at 5:15 A.M. At 6:00 breakfast is served and the girls have until 7:30 A.M. to wash, wax and dust their living quarters prior to inspection. Classes begin at 8:00 A.M.

A woman enlistee in the Marine Corps not only receives some drill instruction but also instruction on the history and traditions of the Marine Corps and she takes instruction in subjects such as typing, business English and general office procedure. She receives instruction in swimming, like her WAVE counterpart. From 5:00 until 9:30 P.M. is a free period for preparing for the following day's classes, writing letters and other personal matters.

During these eight weeks of preparation for a Marine Corps career, the trainee is being tested and evaluated for the most appropriate assignment after completion of basic. She is assigned to advanced schools according to her capabilities, the Marine Corps' need, and the enlistee's preference.

After completing basic training at Parris Island the new Marine is granted leave before reporting to a specialized school or to her first assignment.

WAF

The Air Force trains its "young women in blue" at Lackland Air Force Base, a few miles west of San Antonio. This military base of over 3,000 acres is aptly referred to as the "Gateway to the Air Force," because all basic training—men and women—takes place here on a plateau overlooking historic Kelly Field.

Upon arrival, the new WAF is launched on several days of processing before starting the eight weeks of basic train-

Airman First Class in uniform. *U.S.   Air   Force photo.*

Staff Sergeant in uniform. *U.S. Air Force photo.*

Airman First Class in casual uniform. *U.S. Air Force photo.*

ing. She will be issued a set of smart dark blue uniforms which feature a double-breasted, semi-box jacket with an A-line skirt. It is worn with a light blue blouse, which is complimented by a dark blue tab at the collar. The authorized uniforms for various occasions now consist of slacks, windbreakers, wraparound skirts, and even a floor-length side-split evening skirt.

After completion of processing activities her formal instruction begins. Briefings are received on career opportunities, and instruction on a wide range of subjects, among which are the woman's role in the Air Force, communicable diseases, group living and teamwork, illegal or improper use of drugs, military law, ground safety and driver responsibility, moral lectures, personal affairs, physical conditioning, and personal development. In addition, WAF enlistees are taught the history and traditions of the Air Force and receive a charm and personal hygiene course. The personal hygiene course provides instruction in poise, posture, wardrobe planning, application of makeup, proper diet, attractive hair grooming and etiquette.

Upon graduation, the WAF will report directly to one of the worldwide Air Force installations for her first assignment.

Advanced training could be in management, education and training, medical or dental, personnel, or special services. It depends not only on the enlistee's abilities, but also her desires coupled with the current job openings in the Air Force.

Graduation day is marked by a dress parade in which the recruits "pass in review" before the commander of the school. After that parade the young ladies are no longer recruits and have become full-fledged members of the armed forces.

They recapture their "freedom" and must now accept full responsibility for themselves and prepare to take over jobs that are vital to the security of the nation. From now on responsibility will rest on their shoulders and opportunity for promotion and further training is waiting.

CHAPTER 6

Careers in Administration, Finance, and Data Processing

Once basic training is completed the young enlistee finds a maze of roads leading to many different kinds of careers in the armed forces. Which road to take depends on the choice of a specialized field. For some it will mean disappointment because aptitude tests will show that despite her desire, the career a girl wants is not the one that would bring satisfaction and happiness. The armed services try their best to put the individual where she is needed and where she will do the best job. These things are essential to happiness in a career. In each job area the opportunity for advancement is the same because every career field is important to an efficient organization.

The fields are numerous and each has a number of different jobs. Most of these jobs are found in civilian life. Quite a few of them are difficult to get into in civilian life because they are learned by apprenticeships, or there are few schools that teach the speciality. Thus, training in the armed forces is often the only way a person can get the qualifications needed.

The fields of administration, personnel, finance and data processing are the most open and lucrative fields available to girls entering the work force today. The demand for women is higher in these fields than any other. The Department of Labor reports that approximately 200,000 stenographic-secretarial, 25,000 receptionist, 50,000 typist and thousands of data processing openings occur each year.

Each of the broad categories have many specific jobs. In the armed forces *administrative field* are the secretaries, typists, file clerks, postal clerks, and even court reporters, a specially trained individual who attends and takes dictation at military court-martials, just as a clerk would at a trial in a civilian court trial.

Some of these jobs rate high as glamour spots. For example, an enlisted woman from each of the uniformed services acts as a receptionist for the Secretary of Defense in the Pentagon. These receptionists meet and greet everyone from the President of the United States, heads of foreign countries, U.S. senators, and congressmen and famous people such as entertainers and other celebrities.

A young lady interested in people, their problems, and their ambitions will find *personnel* a fascinating and rewarding field. Personnel specialists greet newly arrived personnel (both officer and enlisted), arrange their job assignments, keep their records, and handle their housing, transfers, leave of absence (vacations), and any problems that come up in regard to employment in the U.S. armed forces. The work is similar to that done by a personnel office in a large business.

The *finance, accounting* and *auditing* fields are for people who enjoy working with numbers, preparing budgets, computing payrolls and handling money. Two examples in this

Airman First Class at her job in the administrative offices. *U.S. Air Force photo.*

field are the *budget specialist,* who assists in planning the budget of her organization and the *payroll clerk,* who computes the pay of the people in the organization and sees that they receive their pay.

The *data processing field* is one of the fastest growing occupational fields and offers unlimited opportunity in business and government. These jobs require a talent for details and the ability to plan a complicated task for a computer. This machine does in minutes a job that would normally take many people days to do. The armed forces pioneered in data processing and they are the world's largest users of computers.

ADMINISTRATIVE

The *administrative field* is the largest career field found in each of the Services. The majority of civilian jobs for women are also in the administrative field. The Department of Labor estimates 2.4 million civilian jobs in this field and that 95 percent are filled by women. These specialists hold any business organization together. The armed forces could not operate without their file clerks, stenographers, typists, and office managers. These administrative types are found in every major career area, such as legal, technical, scientific, medical, intelligence, special services, and infor-

Airman at work in data systems. *U.S. Air Force photo.*

mation. Every office has some clerical work and often it is the girls in uniform who provide it.

In this field the top job is the office manager, who is likely referred to as the NCOIC-Administration—Non-Commissioned Officer in Charge of Administration. That person would be called an office manager in civilian life. A competent office manager must know more about the intricate office operations than the boss, who depends on this individual to keep the workload flowing smoothly. These are the people who know how to get things done and are depended upon to get them done right. Good organizers and leaders with this type of experience are in demand as office managers in business firms.

The typist is to an office what the infantryman is to an army. She may work her way to the top from this job as she learns procedures, filing, and office management. She usually starts out with jobs such as typing reports. Depending on her assignment, these reports might be to a Company Commander, to the Commanding General of an army, to the Secretary of Defense, or in some cases to the President. She could very well type letters or memorandums from high officials to go to the Director of the National Aeronautic and Space Administration (NASA) regarding the astronaut program, or perhaps she might assist in researching and typing an answer to a congressman's request for information about one of his constituents.

She files all information pertaining to her office for future reference and research. She often serves as the office receptionist, answers the phone, and keeps a calendar for her boss and other members of the office staff. She does all secretarial duties with the exception of taking shorthand. There are programs for which she can apply to get additional training in this field, including shorthand. This training might be during or after duty hours. High school courses in English, typing and business are good preparation for this type of job.

Basically, the armed forces will provide training in typing, general office procedures, filing and maintenance of records. The Army teaches typing, shorthand, English composition, filing, and general administration in an eight-week course at Fort McClellan. The Navy trains their administrative personnel either on the job or at schools located at San Diego, California, or Bainbridge, Maryland. The administrative course is thirteen weeks long. The Navy also trains administrative personnel in the technical field of naval aviation. This training is conducted at the Naval Air Technical Training Center, Memphis, Tennessee. The Marine Corps offers an additional course in administration at Parris Island, South Carolina, and trains some of their administrative personnel on the job. The Air Force teaches administration in a twelve-week course in typing, English, and filing at Keesler Air Force Base near Biloxi, Mississippi.

Civilian training courses for a typist may cost as much as $500. To take a very basic secretarial course, excluding shorthand, costs approximately $700. With shorthand, the usual cost is at least $1,000.

A qualified typist in civilian life can make up to $7,000 per year. An experienced secretary can earn anywhere from $6,000 to $9,000 a year, and $12,000 in some civil service positions. Court reporters earn anywhere from $7,000 to $10,000 a year. Office managers are paid from $7,000 to $10,000 a year in a small firm and a higher salary in a larger corporation.

PERSONNEL

A *personnel* specialist works with paper and records, but essentially with people. She is one of the first people a newly enlisted member meets, and probably the last person they will see when leaving the armed forces. Her day-to-day work will include interviewing the new member of an

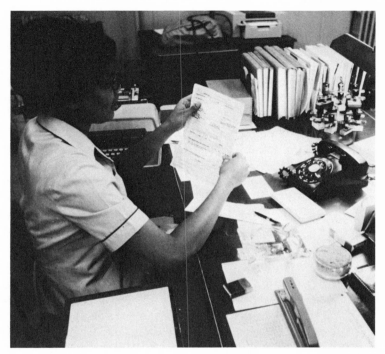

A WAVE prepares a form in the fiscal office at the Naval Schools Command. *U.S. Navy photo.*

organization to obtain information regarding the previous work experience, educational background and interests. At basic training centers this information will help her make recommendations as to the proper career field and assignment. Interviewing job applicants is an art that cannot be easily mastered, but if she has a genuine interest in people she will do well in this type of work.

Personnel work can be satisfying and interesting. It is a job of great responsibility because it is really helping people plan their working lives. The suggestions that personnel specialists make can contribute much to the molding of a

person's future. One of the most important things a member
of the armed forces has is his or her personnel file. It goes
along to each assignment and the information in it is used
to determine future jobs and promotions. It is the job of the
personnel specialist to keep these records up-to-date and
accurate. These records include orders, personal affairs
arrangements, promotion progress, leave requests, transfers, education progress, medals awarded and test results.

Other duties are job analysis and evaluation. The personnel specialist does job analysis through interviews, question-
naires, and by referring to prior research. In the event a
new position is established, she determines what is done,
how it is done, the experience needed, training required,
and related fields. Another part of her work is helping the
individual servicemen and women with their personal
affairs problems such as life insurance beneficiaries, health
and veterans' benefits. In the course of her work the personnel specialist utilizes many different office machines, such as
the electrical scoring machine, the calculator and the typewriter.

Personnel specialists are trained in typing, filing, personnel record keeping, personnel data systems, and key punch
machine operation. In addition, they are taught how to plan
a career development program, and the intricacies of personal affairs management, such as insurance programs,
social security benefits, retirement and estate planning.

The Army trains its personnel specialists at various installations across the country in Kentucky, New Jersey,
California, and Louisiana. Duration of the training is four
weeks. The Navy trains its personnel experts for eight
weeks at either Bainbridge or San Diego. The Marine
Corps trains people in this field at Parris Island, in a six-
weeks course. The Air Force trains its personnel specialists
at Keesler Air Force Base, Mississippi, for twelve weeks.

With experience gained in managing the personnel problems of a few hundred people or of a division of over

15,000 men and women, a woman could adapt easily to the personnel procedures and problems of many civilian concerns, whether it be a local department store or a chain of beauty salons.

The civilian training in this field is either at the college level or during on-the-job training. Trained people in the personnel field are currently earning anywhere from $7,000 to $12,000 a year, as interviewers, job analysts, managers, and vocational advisors.

A seaman works as technician in the data processing department of U.S. Naval Air Station, Alameda, California. *U.S. Navy photo.*

FINANCE

The specialists in the field of *finance* deal with money, from a few dollars to budgets of several billion dollars. Finance, accounting and auditing experts must be able to operate printing calculators, card punch machines, adding machines, comptometers and typewriters. In specialized training, the young woman in uniform learns the rules of basic accounting and expense and ledger systems. In a small unit she must maintain pay records, determine the amount of paychecks, and make up the payroll. Her accuracy and speed are critical because an error in a person's paycheck can have a serious effect on an individual's plans and home life. A finance clerk also prepares and processes claims for reimbursement for travel expenses, reenlistment bonuses and a host of other things that are much like those done by the accounting and controller offices in a civilian business.

It is possible that she could participate in the initial planning of a new million dollar defense project, or compute the possible costs for research, development, and building of a new fighter aircraft, ship, tank, or a space program. She could assist in preparing her organization's part of the budget that the President presents to Congress each year. After congressional approval she may help put the authorized money to work. Since every dollar spent on defense must be carefully recorded and frequently audited, finance is a career field that requires careful and meticulous people to plan for, spend, record the money spent, and analyze the results. This information must be justified on various documents and reports that altogether portray the Defense Department's share of the national budget. In 1970 the Defense Budget was approximately 77 billion dollars.

The Army trains finance specialists in an eight-week course at Fort Benjamin Harrison, Indiana. The Navy trains its finance clerks at Newport, Rhode Island, and San Diego for a period of eleven weeks. The Marine Corps sends its girls to Camp Lejeune, North Carolina, for five weeks of training, and the Air Force trains its girls at Sheppard Air Force Base, Texas, in a ten- to twelve-week course of specialized training.

In the business world, trained specialists in the field of finance are always in demand as payroll clerks, bookkeepers, and junior accountants. These jobs pay anywhere from $5,000 to $10,000 annually, depending upon the firm, the job and the years of experience of the individual. Training in a business school or junior college in this field costs as much as $2,000. A small percentage are trained on the job. The Department of Labor estimates 75,000 job openings in this field every year.

DATA PROCESSING

The field of data processing holds one of the brightest futures of any career field to open for women in recent years.

Women make excellent data programmers because they are generally more meticulous in their work than men. It is now possible through the use of computers to obtain information in a matter of minutes on thousands of subjects. For example, suppose the Secretary of the Army wanted to know how many men had been discharged for medical reasons since January 1, 1950. The program specialist would load her machine with the right combination of cards, and in a few minutes come up with the correct answer. This type of research previously required untold man-hours. However, these timesaving machines are useless without their masters, the programmers.

Computer people have an expression—GIGO—which stands for "garbage in, garbage out." This is a humorous way of saying that the computer's output is no better than the person who told it what to do and how to do it.

Making the machine understand what it is being asked for is the job of the programmer. Although computers do fantastic feats, they are only electronic robots and must be coaxed by a special computer language. Data processing specialists learn this language and must not only operate the data processing equipment, but must prepare the data that goes into the computer. They operate data transceivers, sorters, reproducing machines, interpreting machines, and digital electronic data processing machines. It is a world of hums, whirling tape drums, flashing colored lights and high-speed printing machines that type out the results of the computer's calculations in seconds.

Algebra and math are high school courses that are basic for preparing for a career in this field.

The Army trains its specialists at Fort Monmouth, New Jersey; Fort Benjamin Harrison, Indiana; and Fort Devens, Massachusetts. The course lasts anywhere from five to twelve weeks. The Navy trains its data processors at San Diego for twelve weeks. The Marine Corps sends its girls to either Quantico, Virginia, for six to thirteen weeks or to Sheppard Air Force Base, Texas, for four weeks. The Air Force trains its data processing experts at Sheppard Air Force Base, Texas, for four to twelve weeks.

Civilian programming jobs pay from $7,000 to $12,000 per year with two years experience on the job. Supervisors earn over $17,000 a year. This is with no previous college education. With a college education in mathematics or computer programming, the opportunities in this field are practically unlimited. It is not unusual for programmers to triple their salary in two to three years. With the experience gained in the armed forces a trained person can easily step into a job paying $8,000 to $10,000 a year without the necessary two to three years of on-the-job experience. The cost of civilian training in this field is $1,500 to $2,000.

CHAPTER 7

Careers
as a Medical Assistant,
Laboratory Technician,
Dental Assistant,
and Therapist

From the earliest points in recorded history women have traditionally been the nurses, caring for the young and the sick. It is sometimes called a "woman's instinct." Patients find it soothing and comforting to be nursed by an understanding feminine hand. And women gain great satisfaction from this type of work. This is why so many women choose nursing and related jobs in the medical field.

In civilian clinics, hospitals, laboratories, research institutions, government agencies, and doctors' offices across the nation there is an increasing demand for women trained in medically related skills. These are skills of the medical assistant, physical therapy assistant, operating room assistant, clinical specialist, eye-ear-nose-throat specialist, neuropsychiatric specialist, social work/psychology specialist, optical laboratory specialist, pharmacy specialist, dental laboratory technician, dental assistant, dermatology technician, occupational therapy assistant, and orthopedic appliance technician.

The armed forces must maintain several hundred large hospitals and clinics to take care of the 3.3 million men and women in uniform and their approximately 4.1 million dependents who are also given free medical care. With a medical responsibility as large as this it is necessary to have a substantial number of assistants, specialists and technicians, as in civilian hospitals, to assist the doctors and nurses.

MEDICAL ASSISTANTS

Medical assistants are the practical or vocational nurses in military and naval hospitals and their duties are similar to those found in any civilian hospital. Without them no hospital could give the patients the care they require.

Some of the duties of the medical assistant are giving first aid and doing minor surgery, such as stitching up minor wounds. She applies bandages, dressings and splints. In emergency situations, a medical assistant gives artificial respiration and is trained in the treatment of shock. She gives shots and sterilizes medical instruments for operations. When a patient needs special treatment she prepares them for transportation to another medical facility. She gives patients the doctor's prescribed medication, whether it be a pill or an injection.

She acts primarily as a practical nurse, taking temperatures and recording pulse rates. She maintains all patient records, records that contain details of the frequency of medication, the patient's diet, and reactions to treatment such as fluctuations in temperatures. The records, if kept improperly, could mean the life of the patient. She makes sure the beds are sterile and are made properly for the patient's comfort and attends to the needs of the bedridden.

A medical specialist is trained in a variety of skills, skills she can apply on a job in a civilian hospital or clinic. She is taught the basic principles of nursing, such as recording clinical data, giving medication and therapeutic treatments, collection of specimens, nursing procedures and ward care. She is trained in the use of drugs and antidotes for poison and receives instruction in general first aid such as the treatment of shock, broken bones, choking, wounds, fractures and bites. The importance of sterilization, disinfection and fumigation are taught to her, as well as the different types of anesthetics and how to use them. She learns the importance of a controlled diet and the requirements for certain foods for minimum daily body requirements of vitamins and minerals. She learns and uses special methods of feeding patients, including intravenous feeding. She is taught basic biology, including all the body systems, such as the respiratory and the nervous systems She learns about the various bones and muscles and the part they play in the human body. In addition, she receives instruction on the cells and tissues of the body.

The Army trains its medical assistants at the Medical Training Center at Fort Sam Houston, Texas. This course lasts for eight weeks. Additional training in more technical fields of nursing may be taken and their duration may be anywhere from four to twenty weeks. The Navy trains its medical support specialists at either San Diego, California, or Great Lakes, Illinois, for fourteen weeks. The Air Force trains its specialists in medicine at either Sheppard Air Force Base, Texas, or Brooks Air Force Base, near San Antonio, Texas, for four to thirteen weeks.

The medical assistant can use her skills in civilian jobs such as practical nursing, medical secretarial work, or medical administration. Salaries for these occupations begin at $5,000 and range up to $7,000 a year. The training in this field would cost about $500 in a civilian school and would take approximately six to nine months.

LABORATORY TECHNICIANS

The *laboratory technicians* support the doctors, dentists, and nurses by conducting tests on specimens, such as blood and body fluids, and researching the causes of sickness and disease. Most hospitals and clinics maintain laboratories. In major hospitals these are the work shops of diagnostic medicine. In these antiseptic rooms tests determine whether or not a patient has cancer, a rare disease or a simple virus. The technician's findings form a basis for the doctor's diagnosis and the accuracy of the report often can mean life or death for the patient.

The technician takes blood samples and collects other specimens from patients. She takes them to her laboratory and performs the complicated tests ordered by the doctor. In her day-to-day work the technician must carefully keep records of all her testing and research work. This record keeping is an important part of her job. She is also responsible for maintaining the laboratory equipment she uses.

The girl entering this field of test tubes, microscopes, and slides studies blood chemistry, blood grouping (Types A, B, etc.), hematology, immunohematology, serology, parasitology, bacteriology, and urinalysis.

In order to qualify for the training provided by the services as a medical laboratory specialist it is preferred that the applicant have completed a high school course in either or both algebra and chemistry. However, if a girl shows a genuine inclination and interest in this field every allowance is made to train her in this speciality.

Practically all of the medical training programs are available under the Army's "Choose It Yourself Program." This guarantees training in a particular area before signing the enlistment papers.

The Army trains its laboratory technicians at Fort Sam Houston for fourteen to twenty weeks. Advanced training is

WAC Specialist-5 administers serum to a mouse to determine its reaction to a given disease, as another lab technician looks on. The laboratory is located in Landstuhl, Germany. *U.S. Army photo.*

available in optical and dental laboratory work and pharmacy, also at Fort Sam Houston. These courses last up to fifty weeks. The Navy trains its laboratory technicians at San Diego, California, or Great Lakes, Illinois, for twelve to fourteen weeks. The Air Force trains people for this medical speciality at Sheppard Air Force Base, Texas, for seventeen weeks. Additional advanced training is available at various Air Force bases for a period of up to thirty-six weeks.

If a laboratory specialist should decide to pursue the career in civilian life the need for experienced technicians is increasing. A laboratory technician, with military experience, could as a civilian expect to earn $7,000 to $10,000 a year with a savings in training time of six months and educational costs amounting to over $500.

DENTAL ASSISTANTS

A young woman desiring the crisp white uniform of a *dental assistant* has more than ample opportunity to acquire one in the armed forces. Like medical care, dental care is provided free to all military personnel, though it is not provided normally to their dependents. Therefore, it is necessary to have trained personnel to assist the dentists in the clinics, work in the laboratories, to take X rays and to clean the patient's teeth.

The dental assistant in the armed forces assists the dentist in oral surgery and the routine filling and removal of teeth. She prepares material for fillings and cements for use in repairing teeth. She prepares the impression material that is used by the dentists to make a pattern for false teeth or bridges. She prepares patients for X rays, takes the X ray, and develops the film. She learns the use of more than fifty different medical instruments, sterilizes the instruments and hands them to the dentist as he works. She maintains the

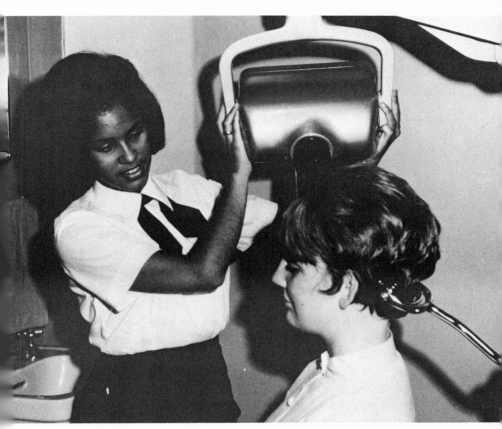

Dental technician prepares to X-ray a patient's teeth. *U.S. Navy photo.*

dental charts on patients and she keeps individual records
on each patient treated. She cleans teeth and instructs
patients in oral hygiene and the proper way of brushing.
Also she assists the dentist in all his administrative and
clerical work, such as keeping the appointment books,
typing reports and correspondence, and filing. She makes
sure there is an ample supply of dental equipment and
materials on hand and helps train girls entering the field.

A young lady choosing this career is trained in many phases of dentistry, as well as in elementary chemistry, anatomy and physiology. She is taught the different drugs used in dentistry and their reactions. She learns how to help the dentist in the operating room and becomes familiar with diseases of teeth, supporting nerves and tissues. In addition, she is trained in the proper way to keep dental records and the upkeep of dental equipment. Also she is instructed in dental health so that she can pass on these helpful hints to patients to possibly help prevent their future need for extensive treatment.

The Army trains its dental specialists and assistants at Fort Sam Houston, Texas. The training lasts from eight to eighteen weeks. The Navy trains its dental technicians for twelve weeks at San Diego, California, or Great Lakes, Illinois. The Air Force trains its dentists' helpers at Sheppard Air Force Base, Texas, for a period of eight to twenty-six weeks.

A dental technician has a job waiting for her if she decides not to make the armed forces a career. Dentists and dental laboratories across the country are in great need of their skills. The time saved by a dentist in having a competent assistant on hand to clean teeth, take X rays, and prepare material for fillings, in addition to having her assistance in surgery, is significant and that is why this type of trained person is in such demand. Some dental assistants name their own hours, work for more than one dentist and practically name their wages.

Dental technicians on the average earn a minimum of $6,000 a year. There are some technical schools in metropolitan areas that will train one in this field for a fee of approximately $600. There are also a limited number of on-the-job trainee positions that become available each year, but this type of training takes as long as four years. There are approximately 26,000 dental laboratory technicians employed today.

OCCUPATIONAL THERAPISTS

Unfortunately, in peacetime as in wartime, there are soldiers, sailors, marines and airmen who lose a limb, their eyesight or their mental faculties. A comforting and supporting arm, eyes, or understanding ear are provided by the *occupational* and *physical therapist specialists* and the *neuropsychiatric nurses aide*. A career in one of these fields requires an extra amount of human kindness topped with huge quantities of understanding. The compassion acquired for the human being while working in these fields proves invaluable in a civilian job as a practical nurse in mental institutions or psychiatric wards of hospitals, or as an occupational or physical therapist specialist in a private or public institution.

In her day-to-day care of patients, the *occupational therapy specialist* contrives games and teaches arts and crafts to ease her patients' tensions. She might teach one patient oil painting and another metal work. She is in daily contact with her patients who not only need medical care, but also understanding and patience to help them regain the use of their body and their mind.

The *physical therapist assistant* is trained in the proper exercise of body muscles. She works daily with her patients to help them regain the use of a limb. With her skillful hands she massages and forces stubborn muscles to exercise until they resume their normal capability of walking, picking up objects or whatever their function might be.

Everyone has emotional problems and some crises in their lives. However, some people are unable to cope with these situations. When the problems become unbearable this is where the psychiatrist and his assistant, the *neuropsychiatric technician,* are needed to help disturbed individuals understand and deal with their difficulties.

As a neuropsychiatric technician, a woman is trained to deal with emotional problems, to administer drugs to com-

A patient in an Army hospital in Frankfurt, Germany, receives instructions in rug weaving from WAC physical therapist. *U.S. Army photo.*

bat depression and given methods of coping with trying and emergency situations. The neuropsychiatric technician in her daily work assists the psychiatrist in his treatment of patients and maintains all the clinical and treatment records. These records are all-important on the day of decision as to whether or not a patient is ready for release.

The training for occupational and physical therapy assistants in the Army is conducted at Fort Sam Houston, Texas, and lasts for four weeks. The Navy trains its assistants in this field at San Diego or Great Lakes for a period of ten to fourteen weeks. The Air Force trains its occupational and physical therapy technicians at Sheppard Air Force Base for ten weeks.

The Army neuropsychiatric specialists are trained in twelve weeks at Fort Sam Houston. The Navy trains its neuropsychiatric assistants at San Diego or Great Lakes for ten to fourteen weeks. The Air Force trains its specialists at Sheppard Air Force Base for six weeks.

Civilian hospitals and institutions always need women trained in these specialities and with armed forces experience they are very much in demand. Beginning earnings range from $6,000 to $7,000 per year. The cost of civilian specialized training is from $500 to $1,000 a year plus additional on-the-job training.

CHAPTER 8

Careers as an Air Traffic Controller, Air Operations Specialist, in Communications and Electronics

Have you ever glanced up into the sky and witnessed what looked like a near collision between two aircraft? Then you surely wondered how these aircraft, flying at 500 miles per hour, managed to maneuver out of each other's way. Actually, they were not as close together as they appeared to the human eye. This control of air traffic in our crowded skies is all due to the excellent teamwork provided by the *air traffic control operators,* whose instructions to busy pilots are relayed by the *radio operators,* their flight plans coordinated by the *air operations specialists,* and the equipment kept in working order by the *electronics specialists.* This team of skilled specialists form the air operations, communications and electronics repair branches of the armed forces. Many work directly with the

Federal Aviation Agency, which controls all flying in the United States, and with control organizations in foreign countries where United States armed forces personnel are stationed.

Without this group's skillful teamwork there would be chaos in the skies; there would be no reliable communications between pilots and the controllers on the ground, and there would not be the speedy communications between military units, aircraft and naval ships protecting the United States.

A girl who has chosen either of these special fields will find herself stationed at one of the Army, Navy, Marine Corps, or Air Force bases throughout the United States. She will be working on the "flight line" and be a part of the glamorous flying profession. She often works under great pressure, but the safety of hundreds of people are in her hands. One mistake could mean a crash or mid-air collision; thus she must remain cool. The duties of air traffic controllers in the armed forces are identical to those of control tower operators at civilian airports. In fact, many of the civilian employees get their training in uniform.

There are numerous jobs within this field that a girl can do equally as well as a man. Some of these fields are: air operations specialist, air traffic control operator, aircraft warning and control technician, communications center specialist, electronic intercept operator/analyst specialist, ground radio operator, Morse code operator, electronic digital data processing repair and aircraft control and warning radar repair.

Trained people are in high demand by the aviation industry, which is one of America's fastest growing businesses. For example, within a decade the number of air travelers is expected to double. Nearly every organization, business or government agency depends on electronic equipment and needs people trained in keeping them working.

AIR TRAFFIC CONTROL TOWER OPERATORS

The *air traffic control tower operator* holds one of the more responsible jobs in the air operations field. This person becomes a set of eyes for the pilot and is sometimes called the "traffic cop of the skies." The air traffic controller literally has hundreds of lives at his or her fingertips, simply because jets fly so fast that pilots do not have time to see each other when approaching head-on at a combined speed of 1,000 miles per hour.

Requirements for this job are stringent. No waivers are granted. An applicant must be in top physical condition, have excellent vision and hearing, be mentally stable, and able to remain calm in an emergency situation. She must be able to read, write, and understand the English language perfectly. Her speech must not reflect any accent, impediment or dialect. This speech requirement is necessary because in her conversation with pilots in the air there is no time to repeat instructions that are vital to the safety of the aircraft and passengers.

In her job as an air traffic control operator at an armed forces base she directs and controls incoming and outgoing air traffic, and ground operations, such as taxiing and parking. She also relays to pilots flight clearances which have been approved by the air traffic control center operated by the Federal Aviation Agency.

Through the use of radio communications, radar, and flashing light signals, she gives the pilot information regarding condition of local air traffic, and his aircraft position and altitude. She informs the pilot of weather conditions, including wind speed direction and velocity, and the pressure reading at her station. In cases of emergency she calls out the fire trucks and emergency rescue squads and calls aircraft specialists to the tower to relay repair instructions to the flight crew. Her orders to pilots are the law and must be obeyed, whether the pilot is a lieutenant or an admiral.

Air Controlman speaks into the microphone as she works in the tower at the Naval Air Station in San Jose, California. *U.S. Navy photo.*

Her eyes are constantly watching the ground traffic awaiting her take-off instructions. From her perch in the control tower high above the airfield, she operates the night lighting controls, navigational aid monitoring equipment, and signaling devices. Also she adjusts and operates radar gear.

During her training in this field the subjects she will study are varied. She is instructed in airport traffic control, air traffic control, air traffic rules, radar approach control and navigational aids. She also learns how to recognize aircraft and understand their performance peculiarities, in addition to weather and radio procedures.

The Army trains its control tower operators in fifteen weeks at Fort Rucker, Alabama. The Navy trains its girls at

Glynco, Georgia, for twelve weeks for the job of air control-man. The Marine Corps also trains its girls at Glynco for sixteen weeks. The Air Force prepares its female air controllers at Keesler Air Force Base, Mississippi for a period of sixteen weeks.

With air travel already the principal form of transportation today, the jobs in this field are plentiful. Anyone trained and experienced in this career might work for the Government as an air controller, as an airport control operator, or an airplane dispatch clerk for an airline. There are technical airline schools that train in this field. The cost would run approximately $1,000. Salaries for these positions range from $8,000 to $17,000 a year depending on the amount of traffic and size of the airport.

AIR OPERATIONS SPECIALISTS

Aircraft do not just fly in and out of airports at the whim of the pilot, especially a pilot in the armed forces. First of all he must have a mission. It might be flying a fighter to intercept an unidentified airplane from over the North Pole, transporting supplies and troops, or just maintaining flight proficiency. Regardless of the mission, the flight must be scheduled and processed for flight clearance. This is the job of the *air operations specialist,* who works in the flight operations office. She is a dispatcher, but her job is much more complicated than, for example, a dispatcher in a truck terminal. The pilot contacts her either by telephone, radio or telegraph, and gives her his proposed flight plans. She then processes his request for clearance. This takes place in several different steps. She checks the flight time en route, the fuel required, the predicted weather, plus the number of passengers and pounds of freight, and compares the request with other outgoing or incoming flights moving at that time. She makes sure that all aircraft flying regulations are being followed. When she has determined that everything is in order she submits the completed request to the clearing authority—the operations officer. When it is approved she contacts the pilot and gives him his clearance and special instructions. Then she makes the proper entries in a log that she keeps to monitor the movement of aircraft and usually on a large bulletin board in the office. On this she keeps up-to-date records of the location of all aircraft en route to the airfield, and aircraft assigned to that base. There is the possibility that she will have the thrill of coordinating the flight plan of "Air Force One," the presidential plane.

The air operations specialist receives training in airspace management, basic theory of flight, rules and regulations governing flight operations, weight and balance of aircraft, weather, map reading, and navigation methods.

The Army trains its air operations specialists at Fort Rucker, Alabama, for five weeks. The Navy and the Marine Corps train their flight operations specialists at Glynco, Georgia, for twelve weeks. The Air Force training in air operations is at Keesler Air Force Base, Mississippi, for three weeks.

Girls accomplished in this field usually find it rather easy to get a job at an airport or with an airline as an aircraft log clerk, flight scheduler, flight planner, or stewardess. The Air Force is the only service which has a specialist category that is much like that of an airline stewardess. This is part of the air operations specialist category.

The practical experience and expert training gained by several years in the service are invaluable if the young woman does not choose to make the armed forces her career. Just like any other job, most employers want experienced people and this is especially important when dealing with such critical work as planning flight schedules.

COMMUNICATIONS SPECIALISTS

The field of communications contains many specialities. Some of these are the jobs of the *communications center specialist, electronic intercept operations specialist, ground radio operator, teletypewriter operator,* and *Morse Code intercept operator.* The communications jobs that are usually filled by women are those of the ground radio operator, teletypewriter operator, and Morse Code intercept operator. The vast communications network of the armed forces requires the support and skill of thousands of these specialists in order to operate twenty-four hours a day. Without their skills the transfer of information would be paralyzed. The prerequisites in this field are those of normal hearing and eyesight plus the ability to learn Morse Code. In addition, these women should be able to type while taking a message over the phone or by dictation.

Messages—similar to telegrams—come in either over the radio or over a wire system like Western Union. There are certain procedures that must be followed when transmitting and receiving these messages. Following these steps correctly and speedily is the job of the communications center specialist. She determines the importance of a message's contents, its security classification and its priority among messages going to the same area or destination. This information is normally a part of the message, but if not it is her job to determine it and to take the necessary action to protect security. Many of these messages are highly classified and their immediate routing to the proper office is essential. An example of this would be a message to the President telling him that a United States ship or airplane had been attacked. Speed is essential in such a situation and it is the specialist who must make sure that the message gets to whom it is addressed as soon as possible.

She must log the messages in a record book, prepare enough copies for all the necessary people, and see that it is delivered. In her work she may operate a teletypewriter machine to transmit messages; she often operates telephone switchboards and other machines in a major communications center. She may also tune radio receivers and transmitters and frequently fixes the more common radio failures.

Her training consists of instruction in typewriting, International Morse Code, radioteletype communications, radio telephone communications, basic electricity, basic electronics and communications equipment circuitry, teletypewriter, security classifications and proper methods of handling classified material. She also learns tape reading and tape relay procedures that are used on the teletypewriter machines.

The Army trains its communications center specialists at Fort Gordon, Georgia, for twelve weeks. The Navy trains its girls for this job at either San Diego, California, or Bain-

Seaman Apprentice sends a radio message to a ship home-ported at Alameda, California. *U.S. Navy photo.*

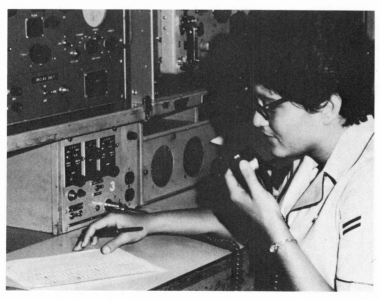

Rerouting message center at Pirmasen, Germany, which receives messages from the European Network for world-wide distribution. *U.S. Army photo.*

bridge, Maryland, for fourteen weeks. The Marine Corps trains its girls in the field of communications at the Marine Corps Recruit Depot, San Diego, California, for eight to twenty weeks. The Air Force trains its communications center specialists at Sheppard Air Force Base, Texas, for thirteen weeks.

The communications network across the nation is increasing in size each year. Naturally this increase brings about the need for more specialists in this field. This is where the girl who has training in this area is a vital asset to airports, radio stations, television stations, Western Union and the telephone companies in every state. In a technical school her training in this field would last almost a year and would cost $600 to $1,000. However, with her military training and several years of experience she could step into a job earning about $5,000 a year.

ELECTRONIC REPAIR

The electronic marvels of today are employed extensively both on the ground and in the air by all the services. To keep these intricate radio, radar and television systems working there must be trained technicians to install, test, repair and perform general upkeep. This is the job of the technicians.

Surprisingly enough a lot of women are now in this field. Women have a knack for working with intricate wiring and equipment. One important requirement for this job is mechanical ability. Also necessary is an analytical mind and reasoning ability to find the cause for malfunctions. The technician must be able to understand technical instructions, possess good vision, and have excellent eye-hand coordination. She must be above average in arithmetic ability and have normal color vision.

Her daily work will consist of making repairs on all types of radar, radio and electronic equipment. She will analyze equipment, test, and replace defective parts. This is a precautionary action before the equipment begins to break down. She also repairs motor systems that provide the power supply, and adjusts and tunes equipment through the use of small tools and testing devices. Training consists of the basics of alternating and direct current, radio theory, prediction charts, electrical testing devices, fundamentals of generators and motors, entries in electronics records, loran, beacon and altimeter systems, airborne radio compass, search and Identification, Friend or Foe (IFF) principles and maintenance skills.

The Army trains its electronics specialists at Fort Gordon, Georgia, for seventeen weeks. The Navy trains its girls in this field at either San Diego, California, San Francisco, California, or Great Lakes, Illinois, for thirteen weeks. The Marine Corps trains at San Diego, California, for six to twenty-eight weeks. The Air Force trains its girls at Keesler Air Force Base, Mississippi, for thirty-five weeks.

WAC works alongside an enlisted man to learn teletype equipment repair. *U.S. Army photo.*

Similar jobs in civilian life are those of the radar mechanic, radio and television repairman and electronics technician. Training for these positions usually takes two years and would cost a minimum of $1,500 to $2,000. This highly specialized field is constantly in need of capable skilled workers. It is the type of skill that could enable one to start their own business at home, such as a TV/radio repair shop in the basement. Many jobs are available with industries of all kinds and with the Federal Government, such as possibly a job with NASA working on the electronic machines supporting the space program. With the population of the United States at over 200 million and every family having at least one or two television sets and at least one radio, the repair service business will need more and more trained people in the future.

CHAPTER 9

Careers as an Intelligence Specialist, Language Specialist, Photo Interpreter, and Weather Specialist

Nathan Hale was the most famous American spy in the Revolutionary War, primarily because he was caught and hanged.

Lydia Darragh was not caught; however, she was a very important intelligence operator during the American Revolution. On the freezing night of December 3, 1777, near Philadelphia, Pennsylvania, she warned General George Washington of the British plans for an attack on Valley Forge. She sent him the number of enemy troops and cannons by means of her needlework—sewing a code into small pockets that gave him the information. The Civil War also had its intelligence agents. Belle Starr, who later became a notorious outlaw, reportedly signalled General Stonewall Jackson by running across a field waving her bonnet.

Methods of getting information on the enemy have much improved today. The data is more complex and communicating the information is much more sophisticated. In every war women have played espionage roles. Some have lived to tell of their exploits while others have been executed for their daring, such as Mata Hari, a German agent, who was executed by the French in World War I. Although the armed forces do not train spies they do train people to evaluate information from a variety of sources, some of which is received from espionage agents.

Intelligence experts in the armed forces have three main jobs: to collect information from radio and television broadcasts, newspapers, and captured documents, analyze it and make available intelligence data. Their function is vital to national security for a number of reasons: to prevent surprise attack, to furnish recommendations on military readiness, and to aid in the preparation and carrying out of military battle plans and operations.

Specialists in this field do their job in several different ways. Intelligence agents, either human or machines, obtain the information. The *translators* and *interpreters* transform the written or spoken foreign language into English. *Interrogators* question prisoners or defectors for intelligence information. *Analysts* listen to radio broadcasts, scrutinize photographs, captured equipment and documents, and written materials for valuable information. The *photomappers* or *mapmakers* construct maps from aerial photos and information from surveyors. *Weather specialists* gather weather information, prepare weather maps, make predictions and give weather briefings. They analyze long-range weather data for operations planning.

INTELLIGENCE SPECIALISTS

The *intelligence analyst operations specialist* has the job of gathering, analyzing and determining the meaning and value of intelligence information. This intelligence information is the data on the present and future capabilities of foreign nations, and present or potential enemies. She makes this data available to those who have a need for such information.

Usually she is assigned responsibility for a foreign country, and becomes an expert through her study and research on its geography, politics, economics, seasonal weather, customs, religions, culture, educational institutions, working conditions, and biographies of government and military officials.

She uses maps, charts, overlays and graphs and researches any data that is available or can be obtained on her assigned subject. She is frequently assigned to special projects, such as selecting bombing targets and aiming points, analyzing the armed forces structure of a foreign nation, or an economics problem of a country. Her job is primarily one of careful and accurate research. It is much like being a detective.

She checks her accuracy with other intelligence agencies and government offices. Once the information is compiled into a useful format, either a report, a booklet, or a chart, it is made available to agencies who can utilize this type of information. In the course of her daily work she could be called upon to prepare briefings for military commanders, pilots, civilian intelligence experts, classes, or groups of government officials.

Intelligence analysts/operations specialists are trained in various skills such as: background of espionage, strategic intelligence, intelligence electronic data processing, photo radar intelligence, maps, charts, recognition techniques, operational intelligence, terminology, languages, research techniques and report writing.

The intelligence analysts in the Army and Marine Corps receive their training at Fort Holabird, Maryland, for ten weeks. The Navy trains its air intelligence specialists at Lowry Air Force Base, Colorado, for fifteen weeks. The Air

Force prepares its women for a career in intelligence at Lowry Air Force Base for sixteen weeks.

With several years' experience and the thorough training provided by the services in this field a girl is prepared for one of several civilian jobs, such as an investigator, statistician, translator, draftsman, topographical draftsman, interpreter, map or chart maker or researcher. Government jobs that are closely related are those of the intelligence research worker and intelligence records analyst. Some of the jobs are available at county or state level, and some with federal government agencies such as State Department, Defense Intelligence Agency or the Central Intelligence Agency. She could also be employed by a private investigating agency.

The training in this field would require several years of on-the-job experience, in addition to technical training. The approximate length of civilian investigating school training would be six months and the cost would be over $500. The trainee's beginning salary would be somewhere in the neighborhood of $115 a week. In government jobs it is possible that she could double this.

LANGUAGE SPECIALISTS

The *language technician, interpreter, interrogator,* or *translator* is a skilled foreign-language expert. She may be called upon to read, interpret and translate a Russian newspaper article, a French newscast or a book written in Arabic. In the course of her work she may be required to monitor foreign radio broadcasts. She prepares translations of captured enemy plans or documents. Perhaps she could serve as a translator for a Communist defector. She may decipher, explain and paraphrase conversations from one language to another. These conversations could be between prisoners of war, deserters, or civilian defectors requesting asylum. Her knowledge of a foreign language could be the link between a confused foreigner and the Free World. Her foreign language skills will be used in many ways, such as translating foreign data on customs of both military and civilian groups of a foreign nation. She may translate information on its technical development. She could even be required to be present at treaty or peace negotiations as a backup language specialist to assist in the translation of the proceedings.

High school courses in foreign languages would prove very useful in this field. However, if a girl shows an aptitude in a particular language or a learning ability in languages she possibly could be trained in this field with no prior language education.

The young woman entering this phase of intelligence will study the foreign language she has shown an aptitude for. In addition, she will be instructed in intelligence reporting, analytical techniques, geography, techniques of interrogation, handling and processing of captured documents, material and personnel.

The Army trains its interpreters and translators at Fort Holabird, Maryland, for twenty weeks. The Navy trains its WAVES for jobs in this field at Pensacola, Florida, for eight to twenty weeks. The Marine Corps trains its translators and interpreters at the Defense Language Institute at either Monterey, California, or Washington, D.C., for a minimum of twenty weeks. The Air Force trains its WAF in this aspect of intelligence at Fort Holabird for twenty weeks.

There are some jobs in civilian life that are closely related to that of the interpreter/translator. Federal agencies such as the State Department, Central Intelligence Agency, the Defense Intelligence Agency, and most large corporations always need people with foreign language ability. There are many companies under government contract to do research work who utilize many people skilled in foreign language. In addition, airline stewardesses flying overseas routes must have a foreign language capability before being accepted for training. Civilian training available in this type of skill is a college course of two to four years' duration, or a special language school. The present cost of a college education is a minimum of $1,700 a year for a state school, and more than $3,000 a year to attend a private college. To attend a language school would cost a minimum of $1,000.

However, without this college training and with the practical experience gained in the service the language specialist could begin earning $6,000 per year.

PHOTO INTERPRETERS

The *photo interpretation* and *photo-mapping specialists* sometimes mean the difference between life and death for combat pilots. It is these sharp-eyed intelligence analysts who spot the surface-to-air missile sites, the antiaircraft sites and the camouflaged enemy jet fighters before they have the chance to attack our ships, aircraft and men. It is also these skilled technicians that can take a photograph, interpret its meaning and from it select targets and make accurate maps leading to the target. In World War II it was a woman photo interpreter in the Royal Air Force who discovered from photographs that the Germans were developing the "buzz bomb" and jet fighters.

The expert in this area analyzes both air and ground photographs. She receives photos, evaluates them, classifies them and files them for future reference. From these she can determine the type of airplanes, location of airfields, number of troops, size of bases, location of fuel and ammunition supplies, power plants and vital transportation centers. Information from her careful evaluation is used to prepare reports, maps and statistical charts and graphs. This material is used in briefings of military commanders, combat crews, and possible interrogation of prisoners of

WAC Private First Class works as a photo interpreter in Army Intelligence. Photo interpreters must complete nineteen weeks of formal study and six months of on-the-job training. *U.S. Army photo.*

war. She makes detailed studies and analysis of photographs for historical and future reference. She sometimes constructs three-dimensional models of geographical areas from the photographic information.

The intelligence photo experts are trained in various photographically related skills. Some of the courses she will study are: photographic interpretation equipment, recognition techniques, basic photography and laboratory techniques, use of the three-dimensional stereoscope, mechanics of photo interpretation, industrial photo interpretation and bombardment photo interpretation.

The Army and the Marine Corps train intelligence photo experts at Fort Holabird, Maryland, for eight weeks. The Navy and the Air Force train their girls for this speciality at Lowry Air Force Base, Colorado, for sixteen weeks.

The training a woman receives in this field helps prepare

her for many civilian jobs such as surveyor, topographical photographer, photographer, aerial photographer, interpreter, cartographic aide, picture analyst, photographic laboratory technician, chart maker, or photo editor.

Training in this field is usually found only in the apprenticeship programs unless related courses are taken in college. Salaries for jobs in this field vary, but begin at a minimum of $5,000 and range all the way up to $12,000 per year.

WEATHER SPECIALISTS

Weathermen are often laughed at for their seemingly inaccurate and frequently wrong forecasts. Nevertheless, it is a job that requires skill, sound training and a better than average intelligence. The specialists in this field do all the leg- and brain-work required to complete the necessary research and study that enables the weather forecaster to predict rain, snow or sun for the day.

During her daily work she observes types, elevation, and density of clouds. She determines the visibility, wind speed, temperature, and air pressure. She does this through the use of various weather instruments such as the thermometer, barometer, anemometers, ceilometers and psychrometer.

After compiling all this information she then summarizes her findings, compares them with historical weather records, determines the minimum and maximum temperatures for the period, and files for future reference the data she has compiled. She also helps in the preparation of flight folders, cloud cover charts and other graphic material for the forecaster's use.

The weather specialist receives her training in weather and cloud observations, meteorological instruments, meteorology, plotting weather phenomena, electronic weather equipment, computation of meteorological data, forecasting and briefing techniques, circulation patterns, high and low pressure areas, condensation, structure of the atmosphere, cloud patterns and systems, weather map analysis, teletype procedure, and radar storm detection equipment.

The Army trains its weather forecasters at Fort Monmouth, New Jersey, for nineteen weeks. The Navy trains its weather specialists at the Naval Air Station, Lakehurst, New Jersey, for nineteen weeks. The Marine Corps trains its female Marines in the art of forecasting at Lakehurst, New Jersey, for nineteen weeks. The Air Force trains its women at Chanute Air Force Base, Illinois, for seventeen to thirty-two weeks.

Experienced personnel in this field find many civilian jobs open to them, such as weather forecasters, weather observers, weather chart makers, or flight advisory meteorologists. Perhaps if a woman in this field has a clear speaking voice, clear handwriting, and poise, she would land a job with the local television station as the weather forecaster.

Service training and experience is considered by some employers, especially the Federal Government, as qualification for the job of weather forecaster. Regardless of her civilian occupation after she leaves the service the time in training saved will be several years of college and the cost of training could well be a minimum of $3,500. Her initial earnings will probably be $8,000 per year.

All of these specialists play an important role in the uniformed services. Women are utilized in many sensitive areas. Some compile and give intelligence briefings to American pilots before their missions over enemy territory. Photographs taken by satellites are being minutely examined each day by photo interpreters to tell the nation's leaders what a potential aggressor is doing, such as building a new missile. These and many other highly technical jobs are being held today by women.

CHAPTER 10

Careers
in Procurement,
Supply, Transportation,
and Repair Specialization

Napoleon is credited with saying that an army travels on its stomach; this is as true today as it was back in the Little Corporal's time. Men have to eat, have to be clothed and have shelter along with guns and ammunition to fight against those who would attack the United States.

Just as it is a tremendous job to transport food and other supplies to cities, it is equally as complicated to supply the many bases and camps of the armed forces. And too, for the complex airplanes, tanks and ships, there must be spare parts. This is the job of the procurement, supply and transportation specialists who buy, issue and deliver the materials and equipment the armed forces use. This group also includes people who repair the equipment.

The Defense Department consumes billions of dollars' worth of such varied items as aspirin, boots, blankets, orange juice, and ammunition yearly. These supplies must be available where they are needed and kept in working order. Keeping the armed forces clothed, fed, housed and armed is the job of buyers—procurement specialists—who must know how to prepare equipment specifications and the invitations to bid, in addition to drawing up the contracts for the purchase of supplies. These specialists determine in advance when to order items that are becoming low in the warehouse. At this point the transportation experts take over and make sure the needed supplies get to their destination in time to be of use. Materials that can be repaired, such as pilot's survival equipment, rubber tires, safety belts, oxygen masks, and parachutes are the responsibility of the fabric, leather, rubber and textile repair specialists.

Some of the specific jobs are the procurement specialist, warehousing specialist, supply specialist, inventory management specialist, storekeeper, transportation supply and parts specialist, air passenger specialist, flight traffic specialist, household goods specialist, freight traffic specialist, packing and shipping, parachute rigger, fabric-leather-rubber products repair specialist and textile repair specialist.

PROCUREMENT SPECIALISTS

The *procurement specialist's* job is to buy supplies for her unit. She receives orders for items and from these orders determines what is needed. She researches and collects the information that is required before a decision is made to buy. For example, she might receive an order for 10,000 tropical raincoats. She must then draw up the specifications such as the type of material, sizes, color and style. She does this by reviewing advertisements, newsletters, catalogs from suppliers and manufacturers, and technical publications to decide upon specifications for the necessary items. If an item is needed immediately she sets priorities and deadlines.

After preparing specifications of the item to be bought, she selects a list of possible bidders from directories and publications. She schedules a bid opening and closing date. She prepares the invitations for bid and adds any special conditions if they are necessary.

She takes and makes a record of all bids and upon the selection of a contractor she prepares the contract. These contracts include all the specifications, starting and completion dates, delivery dates and number of deliveries.

The procurement specialist is trained in buying procedures, preparing invitations to bid, writing contracts, keeping records in negotiation procedures and amending contracts, trade practices, salvage and surplus sales, specification drafting, use of catalogs and government and special Defense Department procurement regulations.

Airman First Class checking invoices in the supply department. *U.S. Air Force photo.*

The Army trains its procurement specialists at Fort Lee, Virginia, for four weeks. The Navy trains its procurement specialists at either San Diego, California, or Newport, Rhode Island, for seven weeks. The Marine Corps trains its procurement specialists at Camp Lejeune, North Carolina, for twelve weeks. The Air Force trains its procurement specialists at Lowry Air Force Base, Colorado, for eight weeks.

The training and experience gained in the field of purchasing supplies are both very useful in gaining employment with industry, department stores, food stores, or any wholesale or retail outlet. Civilian jobs that are very similar to that of the procurement specialist are those of the purchasing agent, buyer, supply manager, warehouseman, and shipping and stock clerk.

Specialized training in this field often can be obtained only by on-the-job training. For that reason with the experience gained in the armed forces a procurement expert could step into a job earning about $5,000 a year.

SUPPLY SPECIALISTS

The armed forces consumes an enormous amount of supplies daily. These supplies are in the form of equipment such as typewriters, trucks, ships, aircraft, fuel, food, clothing, medicines, and ammunition. There are many jobs in this field, such as the warehouse specialist, inventory specialist, fuel specialist, and supply specialist.

It is the responsibility of the *supply specialist* to know and keep track of her unit's or organization's supply inventory and future needs. Just like the homemaker, she must keep her cabinets full, and her fall clothing ready and available when cool weather comes around. When the supply of certain items gets low she makes out a requisition for the items. The secret of success in this field is the ability to foresee item shortages and allow enough time for delivery before the supply is exhausted. When she receives the ordered goods she makes out receipts and reports damaged items. She makes sure the goods are stored correctly and protected from theft.

She maintains up-to-date records of all items and conducts periodic inventories of materials. If the material returned to her stockroom is damaged she makes arrangements to have it turned over to the maintenance shops to be repaired. If she finds she has too much of a particular item she returns it to the main supply base, and if it is beyond repair she turns it over to the disposal office.

As a supply specialist she is trained in various aspects of this field. She is instructed in such things as stock classification, stock numbering, stock control, stock record system, storage procedures, inventory procedures, issuing procedures and forms, use of catalogs, and some office machinery operation.

The Army trains its supply specialists in six weeks at various Army installations across the United States. The Navy trains its supply specialists at either San Diego, California, or Newport, Rhode Island, for twelve weeks. The Marine Corps trains its supply specialists at Camp Lejeune, North Carolina, for four weeks. The Air Force trains its supply experts at Lowry Air Force Base, Colorado, for seven weeks.

There are many civilian jobs that are closely related and some exactly like that of the supply specialist in the armed forces. Those are the jobs of the stockroom clerk, inventory clerk, receiving clerk, shipping clerk, stock control clerk, and stock supervisor.

A young woman will find that civilian training in this field is done on the job with a civilian concern. However, with her military training and experience in stock control she is able to eliminate the low-pay trainee period and she usually begins earning a yearly salary of $6,000.

TRANSPORTATION SPECIALISTS

With our armed forces scattered across the globe it is only natural that there must be a large transportation branch of the services. The specialists in this career field perform many duties. It is the responsibility of the *transportation specialist* to schedule, arrange and control the transportation of supplies, household goods and personnel, both military and their dependents.

The passenger and household goods specialist is often a welcomed helping hand to many confused servicemen. She advises them on their allowances for travel for both themselves and their dependents. She arranges to have their household goods shipped to their new assignment whether it be across the Pacific or across the United States. She selects routes, makes travel reservations, arranges for payment of tickets, and arranges for household goods to be packed, stored or transported. After the orders for transfer are received she is the one who takes care of all the transportation for both officers and enlisted men and women.

During her day-to-day work in transportation she might arrange for a household of furniture in El Paso, Texas, to be stored, and the wife to meet her husband at his new duty station in London, England, where he is being transferred from Vietnam. Obviously, she will have all types of transportation problems to work out.

The passenger and household transportation specialists are trained in military transportation regulations; transportation of supplies and personnel; basic mathematics; civilian air, rail, bus and truck transportation rates; air, bus and rail schedules; transportation forms and the use of some office machinery.

The Army trains its transportation specialists at Fort Eustis, Virginia, for five weeks. The Navy trains its transportation specialists at the Naval Supply Center, Oakland, California, for two weeks. The Marine Corps trains its transportation specialists at Fort Eustis, Virginia, for seven weeks. The Air Force trains its transportation specialists at Sheppard Air Force Base, Texas, for six to seven weeks.

There are many related civilian jobs such as reservation clerk, ticket agent, traffic rate clerk, and travel agent. The civilian training in this field would take a year or more apprenticeship training. However, with the several years' experience in planning transportation movements across the world it would enable a girl to step into a job earning possibly $6,000 per year.

LEATHER-FABRIC-RUBBER-TEXTILE REPAIR SPECIALISTS

There are many pieces of military equipment that are partly or entirely made of rubber, leather, and fabric. When they wear out or are damaged by use it is a waste of the taxpayers' money to toss them out and order new ones. This is where the *fabric, leather and rubber products repair specialist* comes into the picture.

As a repair expert she periodically checks and inspects such things as safety belts, shoulder harnesses, soles of boots and shoes, flight suits, parachutes, and life rafts. She cleans and restores them where needed and mends when necessary. Then she tests the object for renewed durability and safety.

For example, a parachute rigger checks a parachute for tears and double checks the quick release assembly and the ripcord. If the parachute is in need of mending she patches or replaces the section. Then she repacks it and tests it again. She works daily with sewing machines, shears, patterns and various technical manuals.

The specialist in the field of fabric, leather and rubber repair is trained in fundamentals of hand and machine sewing, technique of sewing and repair of leather, repair of life

WAVE Reserve recruits stenciling clothing. *U.S. Navy photo.*

rafts, vests, rubberized protective clothing, repair and maintenance of parachutes, drop testing of parachutes, oxygen
systems and similar lifesaving equipment.

The Army trains its girls in the field of repair at Fort
Lee, Virginia, for eight weeks. There is no Navy training
program in this field. The Air Force trains its women in this
field at Chanute Air Force Base, Illinois, for twelve weeks.

There are several civilian jobs that can be prepared for
by experience in this field, such as parachute inspector,
packer, or repairman, seamstress, alteration expert, uphol-
sterer, and leather repairman.

Technical training in this area is hard to find, but some

schools offer seamstress training that would cost approximately $500 and would take about six months. Regardless, a girl with this type of experience could expect to earn $5,000 a year.

Since buying, supply and transportation are a part of every business and government organization, there is a growing demand for the services of people trained in these fields. This training can even be applied by the homemaker as well.

CHAPTER 11

Careers as a Photographer, Illustrator, Printer, and Food Specialist

Some women find that their talents lie in the more technical fields and perhaps some have found that they have mechanical ability. If they have this kind of talent they will find the armed forces has many such jobs open to women.

The technical fields are photography, optical and instrument repair, illustration, drafting, printing, and the culinary arts. All of these technical fields require a keen eye and a deft finger. Fields such as optical repair, printing and drafting also require some mechanical ability.

The women who work in these fields operate motion picture cameras, illustrate recruiting posters, draft construction blueprints, use the intricate tools required to repair binoculars, and plan and cook the attractive and nutritious meals that are served to the men and women stationed across the world.

Some of the specific jobs are: still photographer, motion picture photographer, audio specialist, television camera operator, film library specialist, photo laboratory specialist, motion picture film editor, surveyor, draftsman, map compiler, modelmaker, illustrator, typesetter, photocopy operator, letterpress operator, lithographer, cook and food services technician.

PHOTOGRAPHERS

A field which seems to have a vast appeal for women is photography, the world of cameras, flash bulbs, and darkrooms. The *photographer* uses her skills in many different ways. The photographs she takes are used for historical records, news stories, publicity, identification, portraits, recording significant events, training aids and illustrations.

Photographer's Mate Second Class shoots some film of aircraft at the Naval Air Station, Washington, D.C. *U.S. Navy photo.*

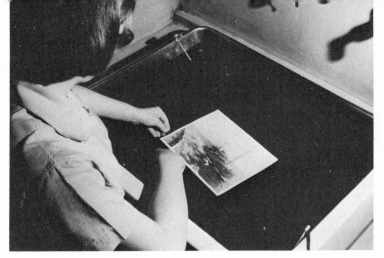

Airman develops a print in the darkroom of the photo lab. *U.S. Navy photo.*

She may be trained in either still or motion picture photography. Sometimes, if she proves her capability, she is trained in both types of photography. During the course of her work she takes both black and white and color photographs. She may be assigned to a public relations office, but is usually assigned to a photographic laboratory. It could be an assignment at March Air Force Base, near Riverside, California, or a photo laboratory on Guam. Wherever she is assigned, she in on constant standby to provide photographic coverage of any important event, such as the arrival of a USO Christmas show or a foreign head of state.

She processes the film and makes the prints of the photographs she takes. She develops the film by using tanks, film trays and photo processing machines. She prepares the developing solutions, times the developing period and then dries the negatives.

From the negatives she makes the number of prints she needs. If she covered a news story such as the moon shot from Cape Kennedy, she might need several hundred copies. She uses contact printers and printing machines to make the prints or photos. After making the first print she inspects it critically, keeping a sharp eye out for blemishes or any unnecessary details. If there are unwanted details she trims the photograph to cut out what she does not want to show, thereby giving it a more professional look. This is called "cropping." If a photograph needs to be blown up to a larger size she uses an enlarger.

She sometimes uses several photographs to make charts and maps. After pasting the individual photos together she uses a copy camera to get a single photo. She also makes minor repairs on her photo equipment.

To become a photographic specialist she must study numerous subjects to prepare her for the job, whether it be working with still or motion pictures. Some of the subjects she is instructed in are basic photography, photographic solutions, photographic chemicals, laboratory and camera operation, optics, exposure and light, operation of developing and printing machines, developing color film, developing motion picture film, motion picture techniques, and mosaic map making.

The Army and Marine Corps train their photographers at Fort Monmouth, New Jersey, for ten weeks. The Navy trains its photographers at Pensacola, Florida, for eighteen weeks. The Air Force trains its photographers at Lowry Air Force, Colorado, for eight to twenty-three weeks.

There are many civilian jobs available to girls with training and experience in this field, such as the commercial photographer, portrait photographer, motion picture camera operator, film editor, news photographer, camera repair specialist, and television camera operator.

The technical training required for jobs in these fields is available only by apprenticeship or college training. Apprenticeships are hard to obtain and take several years to complete. With the armed forces training background and several years of on-the-job experience she should not have any difficulty getting a job starting at $7,500 per year.

ILLUSTRATORS AND DRAFTSMEN

The armed forces need and use a tremendous amount of visual aids to get their ideas across to Congressmen, newsmen, government officials, industry representatives, and to the members of their uniformed services. These visual aids are in the form of training aids, briefing charts, official documents, base newspapers, posters, and various publications. All of these are the products of the skills of the *illustrator* and *draftsman.*

Some of the specialized jobs in this career category are those of the surveyor, construction draftsman, topographic draftsman, cartographic draftsman, map compiler, model maker, and graphics illustrator.

Women in this field find themselves involved in many interesting and productive projects. They work on projects that range from attractively illustrating a recruiting poster to making a model of a new construction project to be used in briefing members of Congress. In her daily work, the illustrator uses drafting instruments, engineering scales, architectural scales, lettering devices and tracing materials.

She sometimes traces drawings and frequently sketches by free-hand copying from objects, specified dimensions, or a verbal description. She uses whatever the job calls for, whether it be pastels, crayons, inks or paints.

She constructs models of terrains, bridges, buildings, towns, base areas and entire military installations. She makes these models with the use of sculptors' hand tools, wood, papier-mâché, plastics, metals, ceramics, cloth and model making machinery.

She also uses her skills in preparing blueprints for the construction of airfields, roads, barracks, office buildings, heating and cooling systems and military installations.

Furthermore, she draws diagrams, charts, and graphs showing trends in all sorts of subjects. These are called "briefing charts" and are used along with a narration to explain to an audience the mission of a base, the status of a study or project or anything that lends itself to graphic illustration.

A woman who likes to draw or was creative in her high school art class is a natural for this field. To become a specialist in the field of illustration and drafting she is trained in many skills, such as: isometric drawing, free-hand drawing, theory of color use, geometric progression, measurement, elementary mechanics, copying methods, fundamentals of drafting and lettering, art layout, elementary algebra, and the reading and interpretation of blueprints.

The Army trains its women in the skills of illustration and drafting for nine weeks at the U.S. Army Engineer School at Fort Belvoir, Virginia. The Navy trains its women in the field of illustration at the U.S. Naval School at Port Hueneme, California, for fifteen weeks. The Marine Corps trains its women in the field of drafting at the U.S. Army Engineer School, Fort Belvoir, Virginia, for ten weeks. The Air Force trains its WAF for duties in this field for six weeks at Sheppard Air Force Base, Texas.

Many commercial industries, construction projects, government agencies, magazines, newspapers, and advertising agencies use the skills of the illustrator and draftsman. Some of the jobs that service training in this field prepare one for are: a commercial artist, model maker, layout artist, draftsman, graphic artist, specification writer or designer.

The civilian training in this field lasts about six months and would cost approximately $600. Of course if a girl is discharged from the armed forces with only the basics of drafting she is not a full-fledged draftsman. However, often the experience gained from a service job of two to four years enables her to get employment initially earning $7,000 per year.

PRINTING SPECIALISTS

Each of the four branches of the armed forces operates its own printing service. The forms used in conducting the paper work of finance, personnel, transportation, general administration, plus bulletins, training pamphlets and booklets, recruiting brochures and base newspapers are all printed by the specialists in this field.

Some of the more specific jobs are those of the typesetter, compositor, photocopy operator, letterpress operator, bindery worker, and the lithographer.

In the course of her daily work a *printing specialist* may have the front page of a newspaper or newsletter to design, which is called "layout." She first selects the size and style of type to be used for both the stories and the headlines. She then decides on the type of binding to be used. The binding selected depends on the publication, which could be folded, stapled, or punched. For a newspaper it is usually folded, and for a magazine it is stapled, but this depends on the number of pages. She jots down these bindery instructions on the front page of her layout. She then turns her work over to the letterpress operator who sets the type and then makes an impression of the assembled layout, which is called a proof sheet.

Reading the proof sheet of her front page she looks for errors, especially in spelling and grammar. If she thinks it necessary, she rearranges the page. Satisfied with her layout she again gives it to the letterpress operator who then turns out the finished product, such as the base newspaper, newsletter or magazine.

A printing specialist or compositor is trained in various skills, such as: the types of paper used in printing, layout techniques, proofreaders' marks, printing inks, use of paper-cutting and paper-folding machines, copy preparation, use of hand-fed and mechanical-fed presses, and other methods of reproduction.

The Army trains its printers at the U.S. Army Engineer School, Fort Belvoir, Virginia, for six to eight weeks. The Navy trains its specialists in printing mainly on the job and at various Navy installations. The Marine Corps trains in this field at Fort Belvoir, Virginia, for eight weeks. The Air Force trains its printers primarily during on-the-job training programs.

The skills learned in this trade enable an experienced person to get a job as a compositor, photoengraver, proofreader, bookbinder, makeup specialist, printer, or on a local newspaper.

Professional training in this field is virtually nonexistent, for it normally requires apprenticeship training. However, with her experience and training an armed services printing specialist could obtain a civilian job that pays initially about $6,000 a year.

FOOD SERVICE SPECIALISTS

The vast numbers of men and women in uniform must eat balanced and well-planned meals. This is not only necessary for their health and well being but it is a big morale factor. In recent years, for example, the old mess halls have been replaced with dining halls which have separate tables with tablecloths and dishes instead of metal trays. They look much like a club or nice restaurant. Food service is now considered both an art and a profession.

The women who specialize in food service do many jobs, such as cooking, baking, cutting meat, nutrition planning, and menu planning. If one is a veterinary technician she is responsible for the inspection and examination of all foods. This is to make sure that they are free of contamination and disease. Without her expertness in recognizing spoiled foods an untold number of men and women could very well be struck down with food poisoning.

An interesting but cold job. Marine checks produce in the cold storage room of the mess commissary storage section at Marine Corps Recruit Depot, San Diego. *Defense Dept. photo (Marine Corps).*

Part of her work is planning the menus and ordering the necessary amounts of staples, spices and meats for hundreds of people. She stores the meats and vegetables so that they are kept at the proper temperature to prevent spoilage. She checks periodically and keeps on hand a supply of linens, dishes, silverware and cooking utensils. She is taught to use the most sanitary and efficient methods of cleaning kitchen ranges, storage lockers, refrigerators, dining rooms, dishes, and cooking utensils.

She might find herself baking bread for an Army division of 15,000 men in North Carolina or cooking a roast beef for a general in Germany. She might be called upon to help arrange a banquet at Fort Myer, Virginia, for the retiring Chief of Staff of the Army. If so, she would make complete arrangements, including floral displays, centerpieces, and special table settings.

She is taught the basics of the culinary art through instructions in cooking, baking, use of dehydrated and frozen foods, nutrition and menu planning, the various meat cuts and grading, the inspection and storage of food, sanitation and pest control.

The Army trains its food service specialists at the U.S. Army Quartermaster School, Fort Lee, Virginia, for eight weeks. The Marine Corps trains its food service technicians at Camp Lejeune, North Carolina, for nine weeks and at Fort Lee, Virginia, for eight weeks. The Air Force trains its food service specialists at Fort Lee, Virginia, for eight weeks.

This experience and training would quite naturally prepare a woman for the role of a good homemaker, school or commercial cafeteria supervisor, cook, restaurant manager, hotel banquet planner, or a caterer.

There are some schools, mostly in major cities, that train students in the cooking arts. The experience and training in the armed forces prepares a woman for a job earning a minimum of $5,000 to $6,000 a year. Some top chefs in hotels earn $15,000 to $20,000 a year. Or if the trainee so desired this is the type of skill that would enable her to earn a living at home by working part time or starting her own catering business. She is well prepared because after all she has learned to feed an army.

CHAPTER 12

Careers in Information
and Special Services

For the woman who wants to be a newspaper reporter, a recreation director, run an employment agency or be a schoolteacher, these jobs can be learned in the armed forces.

These jobs are found in the career fields of *Information, Special Services, Recruiting,* and *Education* and *Training.* These are the specialists who tell the story of what the armed forces is doing, who entertain and recruit members of the armed forces, and who give educational guidance and train people in technical skills.

A specialist in the information field might find herself assigned to work on the base newspaper at Ramey Air Force Base, Puerto Rico. Or she might find herself helping in the arrangements for a national press tour of an underground missile site in Montana. Although she might be responsible only for handing out press kits, she could come in contact with well-known press correspondents and television newscasters.

A specialist in the field of special services might be assigned to a post in Landstuhl, Germany, where she would arrange tours of scenic and historical areas for the military personnel on the post.

If she is in recruiting she might work in an office in Miami, Florida, providing enlistment and reenlistment information for local schools and universities, or even in her own home town.

A specialist in the field of education or training might conduct school activities at an Alaskan base where she would give advice and guidance on educational opportunities, or she might be at Bainbridge, Maryland, training WAVES in technical and semi-professional areas.

All of these jobs call for a genuine interest in people, their problems and ambitions.

Some of the more specific jobs in these fields are: a press information specialist, radio and television specialist, scriptwriter, journalist, radio and television broadcast specialist, physical conditioning and recreation specialist, recruiter, career counselor, educational specialist, audio-visual specialist, and art instructor.

INFORMATION SPECIALISTS

The *information specialist* has one of the most interesting and exciting jobs in the armed forces. It is her job not only to keep her fellow members in uniform up-to-date on world and local happenings, but also to keep the public informed about what the men and women of the armed forces are doing.

As a reporter, for example, she might cover special events such as the launching of a nuclear-powered aircraft carrier. Or she could write news stories for her base news-paper or magazine, and news releases for distribution to the civilian newspapers, magazines, radio and television. She edits her own copy by checking the spelling, correctness of grammar, the accuracy of the facts and the style.

She helps put together the base newspaper by writing columns, stories and features. She works closely with the photographers to get photographic coverage of all news events. She researches historical materials and files and writes updated histories of her organization's activities. She prepares fact sheets and press kits for information handouts to the public. She sometimes writes radio and television scripts for use on Armed Forces Radio and TV networks across the globe. She answers the questions of local news-paper reporters, national newspaper correspondents, maga-zine writers and radio and television newscasters. She ar-ranges press interviews with members of the armed forces. She assists authors in researching material for their books about different aspects of the armed forces. She sometimes helps commercial film companies make motion pictures and television programs about her service. She arranges Armed Forces Day activities and participation in local parades and holiday ceremonies.

For whatever aspect of information work she does, she uses historical documents, files, style manuals, regulations on release of information, and must know copyright and libel laws. She often uses teletype machines and tape re-corders, and of course the telephone, and her constant companion, the typewriter.

To prepare for her job as an information specialist she studies many subjects. Some of these are public speaking, history and organization of the armed forces, preparation and style of news releases, magazine article preparation, radio and television programming, scriptwriting, public re-lations, community relations, newspaper style and format, and radio and television broadcasting.

All of the four uniformed services train their women to be specialists in the field of information at Fort Benjamin Harrison, Indiana, for ten weeks. This is the home of the Defense Information School, and its instructors and faculty are made up of members from all the services.

An information specialist will find that experience in this field opens many doors. Commercial industries, government agencies, individuals and advertising agencies are all trying to get their particular message across to an audience. She soon discovers these doors lead to jobs as newspaper reporters, magazine writers, editors, radio and television broadcasters, public relations writers, historians, research assistants, scriptwriters, advertising assistants, freelance writers, or possibly speech writers in a political campaign or for a corporation president.

College-level training is the only civilian training available in this field. There is some possibility one could be selected for on-the-job training, but this is highly unlikely. If she were chosen it would only come after many years as an impressive and faithful secretary or typist. With her armed forces preparation and several years of experience behind her in the field of public information, a qualified woman could begin earning at least $6,000 a year in a very unusual and fascinating career.

SPECIAL SERVICES SPECIALISTS

Special services is a unique and fun-filled career. It could be a wise choice for the future, because people seem to have more and more free time. To make good use of this free time is the task of the recreation specialist. The women who work in special services are the *physical conditioning* and *recreation specialists* and the *recruiter*.

The recreation specialist's job is to plan for off-duty diversionary and recreation activities for personnel at her

An airman whose job in Special Services (Travel/Recreation/Sports) involves helping organize a talent show. *U.S. Air Force photo.*

location. She does this in a number of ways. She might run the base library at Fort Gordon, Georgia, or be a manager of the swimming pool at Vandenberg Air Force Base, California, or work in a service club in Germany, or plan coming attractions at the base theater for the Marines at Camp Pendelton, California, or manage the hobby shop at the naval base at Great Lakes, Illinois.

She schedules parties, banquets, barbecues, splash parties, hayrides, picnics, dances, talent shows, cycling, skiing and bowling clubs. She must be adept in various hobbies, such as woodworking, painting or ceramics. She must always be ready to help those who wish to learn a hobby. She is responsible for keeping a sufficient amount of recreation supplies, sports equipment, and hobby shop tools and supplies on hand. Her services are for both those in uniform and their dependents.

She organizes shows, plays and all types of stage productions. She advertises for tryouts for parts, giving time and place for auditions. She selects the stars and directs the rehearsals. If costumes are not readily available, she chooses or makes them. She uses what is on hand for making background scenery.

She sometimes makes arrangements for visiting professional talent, singers, bands, combos, comediennes, and USO shows. Especially during the holiday season, such as Christmas, she arranges entertainment of this sort. The happiness a few Hollywood stars bring the uniformed men and women stationed in Korea and other faraway lands are part of her effort. She arranges for the entertainers' transportation, hotel reservations, or government housing and meals.

A woman in the service is assigned to special services from almost every career field. To become a recreation specialist she is trained on the job in various areas such as the basics of service club management, library operation, hobby shop operation, recreation sports, hygiene and first aid, pool management, stage productions, acting techniques, makeup, scenery design and painting. She receives on-the-job training applicable to her job from her supervisor or from other recreation specialists. This is the same in all four uniformed services.

With training and experience gained in this field, women can get jobs as athletic directors, playground directors, gym managers or instructors, hobby shop managers, hobby instructors, stage managers, makeup experts, or as recreation workers in their local hospitals. These are only a few of the opportunities in the recreation field.

The specialized training in this area is largely nonexistent other than through a broad range of college courses. At the present time there are over 45,000 recreation workers employed full-time and another 100,000 employed part-time during the summer; less than one half of these have a college background. Sometimes a woman can receive on-the-job training in this field with a commercial firm; however, with the experience received in the armed forces, a woman should be able to find an interesting job initially starting at about $6,500 a year. The salary range in the civil service goes up to over $15,000 a year and some recreation executives in large communities make as much as $20,000 a year.

EDUCATIONAL AND VOCATIONAL SPECIALISTS

The guidance counselors, teachers and educational administrators of those in the armed forces are the men and women in the educational and training fields. This is a very popular field with a service woman.

She trains other military personnel in various technical fields such as flight simulation, food services, dental laboratory techniques, and instrument repair. She does this through the use of training aids, such as graphic art mock-ups, and instructional films.

Some of the more specific jobs in these two fields are those of the *educational specialist, training aids specialist, projector* and *view-graph operator.*

It is the educational specialist's job to be current on all aspects of the educational development opportunities in the armed forces. She knows the scale of requirements from a high school diploma and the General Educational Development Test, to the requirements for a college degree in law or journalism. She tries to guide people and advise them when they come to her with educational plans or problems.

If a young man should desire to finish high school while in the service she arranges for him to attend classes. When he reaches a point where he can confidently take the General Educational Development Test, she administers the test and grades the results. The same is true for college-degree preparatory courses. She stays aware of the local school offerings in the way of night classes. Many men and women earn college degrees while on active duty, going to nearby colleges at night. Many colleges hold classes on the bases for convenience. She also arranges for authorized financial assistance provided by the armed forces for college courses. She keeps a list of correspondence schools and curriculum that are available for both the technical courses offered by the armed forces, and for civilian schools and college credit courses.

She is trained as an educational specialist primarily on the job; however, various personnel-related courses are useful and her attendance is determined by the job requirements and her supervisor's desires. On the job she is trained in interviewing, counseling, job requirements, educational planning, her individual service's educational programs and opportunities and the veterans' benefits available for education.

The Army trains its career counselors at Fort Benjamin Harrison, Indiana, for five weeks. The Navy trains its educational specialists at the U.S. Naval Training Center, Great Lakes, Illinois, for two to four weeks. The Air Force trains its educational specialists at Sheppard Air Force Base, Texas, for approximately one week.

At the present time specialized training in these fields is available only through college-level programs. However, with armed forces training and several years of experience in the field there are some jobs that the educational specialist would be capable of handling without a college degree, such as employment office advisor, civil service educational advisor, and educational advisor with a commercial firm's personnel office, technical instructor in a vocational training school, a test administrator or a teacher's aide. Jobs in these categories pay a minimum of $5,500 a year.

These are but a few of the jobs available to enlisted members of the armed forces. At the back of the book will be found a complete list.

For more information the reader should consult the nearest large library, most of which keep job handbooks published by the Departments of the Army, Navy, and Air Force.

CHAPTER 13

Officer Training

To become a commissioned officer in the armed forces is a position of high trust, so high that it takes an appointment by the President and approval of the Senate. With a commission a person becomes an "official" of the United States and must live under a rigid code of honor and conduct. Dedication to duty is the basis for everything an officer does—duty to the United States, and duty to the people who are under her command. Not only does the officer lead her people, she must always be aware of their needs and welfare. Being an officer means responsibility as well as authority. Above all it means leadership, because that is what an officer is—an executive who directs his or her organization.

ELIGIBILITY

The young women who seek the gold second lieutenant bars of the Army, Marine Corps, or Air Force, or
the ensign stripes of the Navy must meet almost identical
requirements. The applicant must be a citizen of the United
States to be qualified for a Navy, Marine Corps, or Air
Force commission; however, the Army will consider applications from women who have established permanent
United States residency. She must be single to be accepted
for officer candidate training in the Army. The Navy, Air
Force, and Marine Corps will accept married applicants.

She must have a baccalaureate degree from a four-year
college or university to enter officer candidate training, but
if she has completed two years of college and in addition
has particular military or civilian experience this could be
substituted and she could be eligible, except in the Air
Force and Marine Corps which both require a baccalaureate degree before commissioning. The Marine Corps will
not accept candidates for direct commissions who have
degrees in Medicine, Dentistry, Veterinary Medicine, or
Theology because these Marine Corps needs are supplied
by Navy officers. However, persons with these degrees
could be given Marine Corps commissions, but could not
practice their profession in uniform. For those who do not
have a degree and are accepted in officer candidate school
the armed forces have education programs that offer up to
two years of college training in order to obtain a baccalaureate degree. This requires the officer to serve for a
longer period of time, varying from two to three years,
depending on the length of time needed to obtain her
degree.

The four services differ slightly in their age requirements
for women officer candidates. The Army requires the WAC
officer candidate to be from 20 through 32 years of age, the
WAVE must be between 20 and 27 years of age, the

Woman Marine 21 through 29, the WAF 20½ through 29½ and the Coast Guard applicant, 20 through 30. These age requirements apply to the day the officer candidate takes her oath. She may apply for acceptance as an officer candidate as early as age 18, but cannot enter officer training school until she reaches the minimum age.

Like the enlisted women of each service, the female officer candidate must measure up to very stringent moral qualifications, must pass physical and mental examinations, and undergo a thorough investigation of her past life.

Therefore the officer applicant is not told immediately if she is accepted, but must wait until a National Agency check of her background has been completed by the FBI. It is necessary to have this security clearance in order to work with or have access to classified information or material.

APPLYING FOR A COMMISSION

Assuming that she meets the basic requirements, how does she go about applying for a commission? The application procedures vary slightly between the services. Usually her initial contact will be with the local recruiting office or a nearby military installation. The addresses to write to for officer enlistment information are the same as those given previously for enlisted women in Chapter 4.

The young woman who has decided to apply for an officer's commission will save time by bringing with her the following items: birth certificate, divorce papers (if they apply), transcript of college credits (and if still a student, a letter of verification by an official of her college giving her probable graduation date), and a recent 3-inch by 5-inch photograph (not full length). She will be asked for these items during her initial interview.

At this first interview the recruiter will determine if the applicant meets the basic requirements. If so, the recruiting officer will arrange for the applicant to return at a convenient date for medical and dental examinations, personality tests, and further interviews. In some cases, the interviews are conducted before a review board of several officers from her chosen service.

At the second interview she will complete a personal history form, the Armed Forces Security Questionnaire, provide the recruiter with two personal references (three for the Navy) and two employer's references (all for the Navy). If she has never been employed, two college officials will suffice. In addition, her college dean or an official will be asked to furnish a letter of appraisal.

Throughout these various interviews she is scrutinized closely as to her personal appearance, posture and mannerisms, speech, poise, vocabulary, emotional stability, presentation of ideas, maturity, and other character traits.

MAKING THE FINAL DECISION

Official notification to the anxious young lady will probably be in the form of a letter from the service's headquarters in Washington, D.C. The average waiting period for acceptance of an application can be anywhere from thirty to sixty days.

An applicant is not obligated until she takes her oath. She can change her mind, but if her decision is to go ahead she should contact her local recruiting office or military installation and inform them of her acceptance. They will arrange for her to be sworn in as an officer candidate.

She may choose how she wants to travel to her service's officer training center. If she wants to drive her car, she will be reimbursed for the mileage at the rate of ten cents per mile when she arrives. If she takes her car, she must bring along the current state registration, insurance policy, and title or lien holder information. The car must be registered with the base police force, which issues a decal that permits operation on the base.

WAC OFFICER BASIC TRAINING

The Women's Army Corps Officer Basic Training School is at Fort McClellan, Alabama, where the enlisted WAC takes basic training. It is here that "Candidate _____," as she will be referred to, studies for eighteen weeks in a college-type atmosphere.

Her first week is spent in hours of processing much like those when she registered for college. She again undergoes medical and dental examinations, is given introductory briefings and learns her left foot from her right foot. She meets her instructors and fellow officer candidates. Her name is now on the payroll at $254 monthly.

The wardrobe of WAC officer uniforms are bought with a clothing allowance of approximately $400, which she receives shortly after arrival at Fort McClellan. With this money she must buy two Army officer green uniforms, a blue dress uniform and a beige summer uniform, all complete with matching caps, plus black handbag, cotton beige blouses, black regulation walking shoes and black pumps, a raincoat and an overcoat, stockings, gym suit and gym shoes. Her most important purchases are the insignia and the gold second lieutenant bars. These she will be authorized to wear upon completion of officer training school. During officer training she wears officer candidate school lapel and hat insignia.

The storage space allotted each candidate in the quarters, which accommodate about fifty officer candidates, is limited, so each student is advised to travel lightly. Anything she needs is readily available at the post exchange, which is like any home-town department store.

There are kitchens on every floor of the training school.

Officer candidates find the library contains reference material on almost any subject. *U.S. Army photo.*

Each officer candidate has kitchen privileges and she may have her own coffee pot or teakettle and toaster. There are washers and driers on every floor. Color television and hi-fidelity sets, desks, typewriters, and magazines are provided in the living rooms. Laundry and maid service are available at a slight charge. The rooms are tastefully furnished with drapes, carpet, and spreads. The candidate has her meals with other officer trainees in the dining hall Monday through Saturday mornings. Her weekday evenings and weekends from 12:00 noon on Saturday to Monday morning are free. She may travel within a seventy-mile radius but she must have a pass to remain away overnight.

She should bring clothing that she would take on a short trip, keeping in mind the season of the year. Such items are walking shoes, shower clogs, house slippers, nightgowns, robe, daytime dresses or suits, "after five" dresses, raincoat, sweater, cosmetics, curlers, shampoo, a set of white towels and washcloths, stationery, stamps, pen, sewing kit and alarm clock.

The classes she attends five days a week are conducted like those in college. She studies thirty different subjects, including effective speaking, grooming, the part women play in the Army, techniques of instruction, personnel management, administration, security, map and aerial photo reading, intelligence, traditions, Army organization and its role in defense, Army information programs, communications, supply, weapons, domestic emergencies, nuclear warfare, survival-evasion and escape (techniques to use if captured), and military justice. She also marches and drills for 68 hours of the total 792 hours of training.

Towards the end of the eighteen weeks of drill, studying, eating, sleeping, and learning to live in close harmony with others, the student officer is given a preference sheet on which she lists her four assignment choices. Based on her instructors' analysis throughout the training, and an interview with the career guidance officer, her initial assignment is made. Soon after filling out this sheet she is told of her upcoming assignment, whether it be to her first job or to a training school to prepare her in a speciality. After two weeks of leave she reports for her first job as a WAC officer and junior executive in the Army.

WAVE OFFICER TRAINING

WAVE officers are trained at the U.S. Naval Base at Newport, Rhode Island. The WAVE officer training program lasts for sixteen weeks in this colorful New England seaport.

Candidates spend their first few days in briefings, wardrobe fittings for their WAVE uniforms, medical and dental examinations, arranging living quarters, meeting other officer candidates, testing, filling out forms, and learning the basics of drilling and naval courtesy, such as the hand salute.

Each prospective WAVE officer receives a uniform allowance of approximately $400. At Newport she is fitted for her wardrobe of Navy blues soon after arrival. However, it is recommended that she bring several daytime dresses or suits to tide her over until her uniforms are ready. After alterations are determined, it sometimes takes as long as three weeks before she receives her Navy uniforms. Those she is required to purchase are: summer blues and whites, dress white, the dark blue wool, and the year-round dress uniform complete with its gold braid. All these two-piece ensembles have corresponding hats, gloves, bags and shoes.

Items she might find useful to bring with her are: an alarm clock, stationery, seasonal sports clothing, garment bag, portable typewriter, washcloths, sewing kit, shower cap, shower shoes, and cosmetics. She also might bring about $150 to $175 expense money to cover her needs until she gets her first check.

She will share her room with another WAVE officer candidate, in an atmosphere much like that of a college dormitory. There is a television lounge and a kitchen, and washing and ironing facilities are available. Meals are taken with male officer candidates in the school dining hall at the beginning of the training program. In the final phase of her training she joins male naval officers in the Officers' Mess for her meals. WAVE officer candidates may date during the entire period.

Her first eight weeks are spent in taking instruction in Navy regulations, traditions, history, customs, etiquette, ships and aircraft, weapons and sea power. The second eight weeks are filled with intensive study in such areas as leadership, administration, personnel, naval correspondence and publications, communications, military justice, grooming and the duties of a WAVE officer. During the second eight weeks her class makes various trips, such as to the submarine base at New London, Connecticut, and probably the most exciting trip of all is a one-day cruise aboard a Navy ship.

An instructor at the U.S. Women's Army Corps School instructs an eager group of college juniors in map reading. The women attending the four-week course receive a complete orientation on life as a WAC officer. *U.S. Army photo.*

The officer candidate is given the opportunity to state her assignment preference before graduation. Shortly before the big day she is told where her first assignment will be. After receiving her commission and the right to wear the insignia of an ensign, she is given a short leave before reporting to her first duty station.

MARINE CORPS OFFICER TRAINING

Each summer at Quantico, Virginia, just south of Washington, D.C., the Marine Corps conducts its nine-week Women Officer Candidate Course. After completing this phase the officer candidate goes on to the Women Officer Basic Course, which lasts for seven additional weeks. Thus, she completes a total of sixteen weeks of training before becoming a full-fledged Marine Corps officer. The male officer candidates of the Marine Corps are also trained here.

The Marine Corps officer candidate receives instruction in the responsibilities of an officer, management, administration, leadership, Marine Corps history, traditions and customs, drill, inspection and ceremony, physical fitness, and personal grooming.

A particularly interesting aspect of the training of women officer candidates is the Marine Corps Grooming Laboratory which was begun in 1968. The Marine Corps sent twenty of its women to a famous international airline's stewardess school to see how stewardesses obtain their charm, poise and appeal. When they returned to Quantico, the lady Marines redesigned their classrooms, attempting to give their courses the flavor and atmosphere of a stewardesses' school. Wood-paneled walls, carpeting, and soft lights now set the stage for the making of the woman Marine Corps officer.

Unlike her sisters in the Army and Navy, the officer candidate in the Marine Corps is issued her first wardrobe of Marine Corps uniforms. Her initial wardrobe consists of three uniforms—both greens and whites—matching caps and coats, a pair of gloves and a black handbag, green cotton slacks, two pairs of walking shoes, a pair of black dress pumps, three pairs of stockings, the U.S. Marine Corps insignia, and the second lieutenant bars. After she receives her commission she must add to or replace items in her wardrobe at her own expense. This is true of all four services.

WAF OFFICER TRAINING

Deep in the southwest is Lackland Air Force Base, San

Antonio, Texas, where the Air Force conducts its coeducational officer training program. The prospective male and female Air Force officer trains and studies there for twelve weeks. In its eleven-year history, Lackland has graduated over 40,000 Air Force officers. The first class in 1958 consisted of ninety second lieutenants, twelve of whom were WAF.

On arrival, the WAF officer candidate is met by an upperclass woman who has completed the first six weeks of Officer Training School. These upperclass women show the new arrival her living quarters and teach her the housekeeping duties and the honor system. Her room will be furnished with two beds, a study table, chairs, and dressers. Her guide also instructs her in drilling. Her first few days are spent in physical examinations, orientation briefings and uniform fittings.

The wardrobe of Air Force blues are issued to her approximately three weeks after her arrival at San Antonio. She will be issued both summer and winter blues, complete with a box jacket that has a double-breasted look, and an A-line skirt. These uniforms are worn with matching berets or blue caps, light blue blouses, dark blue tab ties, and walking shoes. Her most important uniform accessory is her array of insignia, including the gold bars that she will pin on her epaulets when she is commissioned as a second lieutenant.

Other uniform items she will wear in her WAF career are wash-and-wear blue wraparound skirts, windbreakers, and pale blue blouses with roll-up sleeves. Some WAF and aeromedical evacuation nurses may wear trim blue slacks. The officer candidate wears, appropriate to her uniform, white, black or blue sneakers, loafers or pumps. For very special occasions, the WAF wear a floor-length (side-split to mid-knee) black dinner skirt. This is worn with a short bolero jacket (white for summer, black for winter), a white ruffled blouse and a silver cummerbund. She may substitute a short cocktail-length black skirt for the floor-length skirt. Daytime skirt lengths are to be whatever looks best on the individual. Femininity is always stressed.

The prospective WAF officer candidate's day begins at 5:30 A.M. After two weeks of satisfactory work she may have an "open base" privilege. This means she can have free time from 1 P.M. Saturday until 6 P.M. Sunday and travel within a three-hundred-mile radius of the base.

She shares her bedroom with another WAF officer candidate and her bath with three other trainees. Because of this semi-community living arrangement, WAF officer candidates are told to bring only the essentials of their wardrobe, including a suit, day dresses, casual and cocktail attire. In addition, they should bring such items as a plastic cup, cosmetics, makeup kit, shower shoes, shower cap, a soap dish with a cover, lounging robe, and slippers. Some optional items to bring are: an iron, typewriter, alarm clock, radio, bathing suit, ashtray, and dictionary. She will have her meals cafeteria style with other officer candidates in one of the several dining halls at Lackland Air Force Base.

Each officer training class is organized as a wing. The candidate thus gets experience in responsible positions in squadron and wing organizations. She attends classes five days a week on a schedule much like that she had at college. She studies such important aspects of Air Force life as leadership, Air Force organization, the United States and world affairs, WAF officer responsibilities, human relations, aerospace doctrine, aeronautics, hairstyling and grooming.

Each new WAC, WAVE, Marine Corps officer, or WAF is placed in a job of responsibility in a variety of career fields. The career fields are diversified in number as well as in subject areas. While she may begin her service period in one career field, she may change this by on-the-job training or by attending a school. One of the truly remarkable things about the armed forces is the opportunity to switch to another career field if one desires.

CHAPTER 14

Officer Career Fields

According to Labor Department statistics, women earn almost 40 percent of the college degrees awarded in the United States each year. The number of girls continuing their formal education after high school is increasing—almost 60 percent enter colleges and universities each fall. However, unless a young female college graduate enters a professional field dominated by women, such as social work (80 percent female) or library work (60 percent female), she oftentimes experiences a degree of job discrimination, although this is forbidden by Federal law. Therefore, she is often unable to immediately utilize her education. Many times college-trained women must take secretarial jobs in order to work their way into the executive level of a company, and then they are not always successful. Even in the field of teaching there is not a large percentage of women in the top management jobs.

This discrimination is not present in the armed forces, for the uniformed services are no longer a completely male-oriented organization. Previous restrictions have been lifted and a distaff officer may now command a base or unit and wear the stars of a general on her shoulders. Lady officers now hold high-level jobs in almost every field, except those, of course, that are related to combat. The woman officer cannot fly a supersonic F-111 jet or command a nuclear submarine, but she can plan training programs for pilots and design new and more sophisticated things such as space stations.

WAC, WAVE, Marine Corps, and WAF officers are assigned to responsible positions in every field open to them. These are executive positions which require not only technical skill but also leadership capability. An officer will have the responsibility of getting a job done, regardless of its complexity or the time required to complete it. She must take the responsibility for failure regardless of who under her command is at fault, because as an officer she is responsible for planning, arranging, supervising and ensuring that a project is completed. This could be a project as vital to national security as the Minuteman intercontinental ballistic missile. For example, a WAF major earned her "missileman's badge" in 1969 for her work in developing this program.

An officer's job, as a member of the armed forces, is comparable to that of a civilian business executive. Officers are the executives of the four services. She could be a biological chemist working on the contamination of space capsules, or she could be tracking and analyzing a space vehicle's orbits around the earth. She could be assigned to the diplomatic corps in the U.S. Embassy in Rome. She might be a staff officer in a protocol office in Washington, D.C., planning the guest list, speakers and entertainment for a banquet in honor of the defense minister of a foreign nation; an intelligence officer studying captured documents;

a personnel officer in Spain or a finance officer in Korea. She might even find herself writing a Veteran's Day speech and arranging a television appearance for her commanding general. The opportunities are there—for the girl who wants responsibility.

Some of the more than thirty career fields she may be assigned to are administration, personnel, finance and supply, transportation, communications, intelligence, air operations and weather, education and training, scientific and technical, public information and special services.

ADMINISTRATION

There are two types of administrative officers: those who direct and supervise the functions of an office (office manager), whether it is an Intelligence office or an Information office which deals with the press, and those commissioned officers who work in the Administrative office. If a woman were assigned to an administrative office she would write, process, publish and make available administrative publications on such things as the proper procedures for handling "top secret" information, and how to prepare correspondence for the Secretary of Defense's signature. She could be responsible for a staff of three junior officers, or a staff of fifty enlisted men and women. Her responsibility depends upon the size and scope of her organization. A degree in business administration would be helpful in this field.

Every office has an office manager. Their military counterpart is the administrative officer. She reads all letters and messages that come into her office or division and determines what her office staff should answer, file, or refer to another section. She is responsible for reports and surveys prepared by her office being submitted on time and she supervises the stenographic and clerical workers, both civilian and military.

PERSONNEL

The armed force's most vital resource is its people. They must be where they are needed, trained to do the job required and satisfied in their work. This means keeping everyone happy all the time, a virtually impossible task, but an important one to morale and an interesting one to tackle.

A personnel officer will direct a variety of tasks, such as handling promotion boards, arranging transfers, selecting replacements, reviewing award or decoration recommendations, or arranging for continuing education programs. The decision as to whether or not an individual should be utilized as an intelligence analyst or a public information officer is often that of a personnel officer, because she is the expert on aptitude tests and personnel management. If she has a degree in business or public administration or personnel management, this is likely to be the field to which she will be assigned at the start of her service career.

FINANCE AND SUPPLY

Keeping the Army, Navy, Marine Corps, and Air Force fed, clothed, armed and paid, and their billion-dollar budgets straight takes someone with competent accounting and planning ability. These are qualities the officer in finance and supply must possess.

As a finance officer she might be responsible for directing her staff of finance specialists in the preparation of a payroll of several million dollars. She supervises the computation of pay and allowances, preparation of paychecks and ensures that accurate records are kept of all transactions. She could be assigned to the management field, evaluating various divisions' requests for money, and comparing these with current budget and future requirements. She would also be involved, in some cases, with planning her service's budget by doing research and analyzing various expenditures. A bachelor's degree in business administration is desirable and college-level courses in accounting are mandatory for careers in this field. However, the latter can be provided for by the service if an officer shows an aptitude.

If she were a supply officer, her job could be a manager of a warehouse or disbursing center, making sure that all requests for supplies are filled properly and on time. She might be in the planning section which studies the current supplies and possible future and emergency needs of her service. She could also be involved in research of clothing and equipment in order to improve inventory and supply procedures. A degree in business administration would be helpful to a woman in this field.

She might be the manager of the post exchange in Ram-

Navy lieutenant operating an IBM computer at Countermeasures Squadron 2, Naval Station, Rota, Spain. *U.S. Navy photo.*

stein, Germany, ordering everything for her store's shelves from hairspray to wedding rings, or manager of the ship's store in Naples, Italy. She could be the finance officer at Don Muang Airport, Bangkok, Thailand. Some women find themselves supervising a staff of over two hundred people and the responsibility of running all the commercially related activities on a military installation such as the post exchanges, dining halls, barber shops, and the interior decoration of office buildings and the enlisted and officers' quarters on the base. In Vietnam one young WAF officer found herself in charge of a computerized logistics operation devised to provide support for Air Force units in that combat zone.

TRANSPORTATION

Providing worldwide transportation services for individual soldiers, sailors, marines and airmen, and even entire units plus supplies and household goods, is the responsibility of the transportation officer. Movement of people and things is a complicated process that must be kept operating smoothly at all times. One wrong decision and a four-star general's furniture could end up on the opposite side of the world, or a battalion could be three days late for a NATO war exercise.

A transportation officer might be at Travis Air Force Base, California, arranging for a colonel and his family to move to Guam. She could be responsible for arranging for medical supplies to reach an isolated base in Alaska, or managing an air squadron's return from temporary duty in Japan. Her travel arrangements cover the entire free world so she must be familiar with foreign airlines, railroads and currency. In her supervision of the transportation specialists who help her she will find a degree in business administration with courses in transportation very useful.

COMMUNICATIONS

The intricate science of sending and receiving information is called communications. It has many forms, from teletype messages, telegrams, radiograms, and photo facsimiles, to instantaneous microwave transmission of radio signals. The officer in this field is responsible for the information being decoded or coded, typed or reproduced in a readable form, recorded and delivered or dispatched to the designated addressee as quickly as possible. The various communications specialists work under her supervision. Her staff may be comprised of teletypewriter operators, switchboard operators, data processors, radio operators or cryptographers who put into code outgoing classified messages and decode incoming classified information. A degree in business administration, physics or mathematics would be very useful and almost guarantee assignment in this field.

In matters pertaining to the defense of the United States this officer's judgment of the importance of a communication's content, whether it be a teletype message received in Bangkok, Thailand, or a phone call taken in the Air Force Command Post beneath the Pentagon, could someday mean the security of the United States or other nations. This is one of the more nerve-wracking jobs in the armed forces, and one that is done on the basis of twenty-four hours a day. Weeks, hours and days sometimes go by with only routine message traffic coming in and going out of her office. Then a vital item begins pouring out of the teletype machine and her job takes on new importance.

During the Vietnam War, a WAF communications officer was the first female in her career field to be assigned to a combat zone. As head of the Base Communications and Data Systems Division for Tan Son Nhut Air Base, Saigon, Vietnam, her primary responsibility was the supervision of the installation and maintenance of telephone and teletype facilities throughout the nation of Vietnam.

A communications electronics officer observing a radar screen. *U.S. Air Force photo.*

INTELLIGENCE

Some of the most thrilling and exciting jobs are those of the intelligence officers. Young WAF officers held meetings and helped to plan bombing missions during the war in Vietnam. Then they briefed the seasoned pilots regarding their bombing targets over North and South Vietnam. An intelligence officer also debriefs aircraft commanders and crews. Another job is the interrogation of defectors, informers, or prisoners. She might also be involved in attempts to break foreign codes. However, her job is not one that can be discussed after duty hours because it deals with highly classified information and her responsibility is the security of her fellow Americans. A degree in psychology or foreign affairs, with fluency in a foreign language would be most useful to an officer in intelligence.

The responsibility of gathering every conceivable piece of background information about a foreign military officer or a new development and putting it into a logical order and readable sequence is oftentimes the short deadline job of the intelligence analyst. Imagine the tension-filled moments and days prior to the announcement by President Kennedy of the presence of Russian missiles in Cuba. If the officer is a foreign area specialist she must be knowledgeable in her geographical area and prepared at a minute's notice to come up with vital security information. Sometimes this information is for the White House Situation Room. For this responsibility she is trained in the language, customs, political, economic and sociological aspects of her assigned area.

She could be assigned as a combat intelligence officer at the North American Air Defense Command in Colorado, carefully monitoring her radar screens and hoping never to see enemy planes swooping in for attack, or she could be a captured document expert responsible for translating a document's contents and analyzing its importance and meaning.

AIR OPERATIONS AND WEATHER

An air operations officer's duties could be in several

Weather officer advising pilot of weather conditions. *U.S. Air Force photo.*

areas of air operations. She could be an air traffic control officer and plan and organize an air traffic control unit. She could be the supervisor and coordinator of the control tower. The air operations specialists work under her direction and supervision. It is her job to give them additional training after they are assigned and ensure that all air traffic is flowing smoothly. She works closely with the Federal

Aviation Administration, other services and foreign agencies on their airspace requirements. She would be better prepared for this field and more confident of being assigned to it if she had a bachelor's degree in engineering with some courses in management and administration.

A weather officer will be responsible for accurate weather forecasts. She will make visual, aerial, surface and instrumental observations. From these she analyzes, describes and develops a forecast of weather. She will be the supervisor of the weather specialists. In addition to her weather forecasting duties she will also brief air crews and other military personnel on weather. This could be in a combat-related situation such as weather briefings prior to an air strike or a troop drop. She could command a weather detachment.

A woman in this field could be the air operations officer in charge of the control tower at busy Eglin AFB, Florida, where an average of 25,000 aircraft landings and takeoffs occur each month, or she could be in charge of the weather forecasting activities at Misawa Air Base, Japan. A degree in science or engineering with at least twenty-four semester hours in meteorology would be helpful in this career field.

EDUCATION AND TRAINING

A popular misconception is that once someone is in the service they learn a job and that is all. Some people believe no further training or education is required and the servicemen are just mechanical robots. This, of course, is untrue because nearly everyone in uniform is constantly taking some type of training. Education and training just begins upon entry into the service. The armed forces are in perpetual need of well-trained personnel in both the technical and professional fields. To make sure there is always an adequate supply of these trained experts the armed forces have instituted various education programs at all levels that benefit not only the service but the individual.

These programs range from technical schools in electronics and clerical schools in typing and shorthand to high school correspondence or college programs conducted on campus. The efficient management of these programs are the responsibilities of the education officer. Her duties range from planning an education program, designing the textbooks, setting up the tests, evaluating the grading system, and developing training devices to actually teaching the course. She will find a bachelor's degree in psychology or education is very useful in this field.

She might devise and conduct research projects on foreign languages and their instruction at the Defense Language Institute in Washington, D.C.; she could also teach classes in English composition or military history at a base or supervise ROTC programs on campuses of colleges and universities.

SCIENTIFIC AND TECHNICAL FIELDS

Female scientists find unlimited opportunity to pursue research projects in the armed forces, from testing and researching the amount of noise the human ear can withstand to designing new missiles and weapons. The scientific field is wide open and the armed forces go to considerable effort to put scientists on research projects. More often than not the scientist in uniform has much more responsibility and freedom to choose her projects than she finds in civilian life.

The scientific field utilizes scientific personnel such as the physicist, chemist, nuclear research officer, behavorial scientist, mathematician and metallurgist. However, to qualify for jobs in any of these areas a bachelor's degree in that speciality is necessary. Later she might be able to obtain a master's degree in that field through service education programs.

PUBLIC INFORMATION

The job of the public information officer could be a combination of social director, newspaper editor, motion picture director, and public relations expert.

An information officer will supervise the managing editors of the base newspaper, sending her reporters (information specialists) out to cover a story that would be of interest to the men and women assigned there. It is her job to decide what is news. She also is the agent or liaison between her base or installation and the press. If there were an aircraft accident or some type of crime on the base her job would be to handle the newsmen looking for a story. She would control nearly any project that involves newsmen, authors, radio and television broadcasters, and motion picture producers. She tries to keep the public aware of what her service and its members are doing. She does this by preparing news releases, photographs and radio and television broadcasts. She would upon request give speeches at local conferences, luncheons or festivities, both on the base and in the local community. She could also be the chairman of her base's reception committee, meeting and greeting everyone from the local Kiwanis Club to the President of the Philippines.

She is the tour director for congressional visitors to the base, or the planner of her service secretary's press conferences. On an hour's notice she could be ordered to any place in the world where her talents in dealing with the press are needed. She might be an information officer for her service's basic training school or on the staff of the Assistant Secretary of Defense for Public Affairs, in the Pentagon, in Washington, D.C. Helpful college degrees in this field would be those of journalism, social science, communications, or public relations.

SPECIAL SERVICES

As part of her job, the recreation director will be making plans for the USO Christmas tour in Korea and arranging the performers' takeoff time to make their curtain call in Honolulu. However, she is referred to in the services as a Special Services officer. She has in her realm of responsibilities the task of providing qualified personnel and supervising their work in such things as hobby instructions, libraries, and recreation programs. She is responsible for the smooth operation of all types of recreation activities from the base swimming pool and library to the service club. She organizes such things as special parties, talent shows, beauty contests, sports tournaments and dances. She has enlisted men and women trained in these areas assigned to her and some civilian personnel under her supervision.

She could be scheduling the motion pictures to be shown in the base theater in the coming months, or she could be scheduling USO shows to go on tour around the world. She could organize tours of all-soldier traveling shows and the various service bands. She could start little theater groups and barbershop quartets. Her job has a big responsibility— seeing that there is something for everyone to do during off-duty time—both for military personnel and their dependents. Degrees in physical education, liberal arts, drama, and psychology would be helpful in this field, but this officer's most important asset is that she must be an expert at devising fun-filled activities.

CHAPTER 15

Nursing and
Medical Services Careers

There are nearly 4 million women in the United States working in professional and technical career fields. Of that number, about one out of four are holding positions in medical and other health fields. Women are heavily represented in the health fields, but only 7 percent are doctors. Traditionally, women have overwhelmingly dominated the nurse career field, although today there are more and more male nurses. But nursing is "woman's territory," as are many other jobs in the medical and health field.

Since the military services have the same needs as any civilian community there must be health facilities such as hospitals and clinics. And since the physical condition of the soldier, sailor, marine and airman must always be excellent if he is to be a good fighting man, the military services practice a great deal of preventive medicine, such as frequent physical examinations, inoculations and physical training programs.

Then there is always the need for the armed forces to be manned so that if war should come they have the facilities to treat large numbers of wounded. Therefore, the medical and health units of the armed forces, in comparison to a civilian community of the same size, is usually quite large. As a result, everyone in uniform is assured of the best medical care in the world, and it makes the armed forces an excellent career for nurses and other medical specialists.

The women who wear the nurse's cap as part of their uniforms are commissioned officers in the Army, Navy, and Air Force Nurse Corps. There are also other women officers in the medical specialists corps in each service: the Army Medical Specialist Corps, the Navy Medical Service Corps, and the Air Force Medical Specialists Biomedical

A U.S. Air Force flight nurse and a Red Cross nurse attend to the needs of American wounded prior to their evacuation from Vietnam. The wounded personnel are already aboard the Air Force C-141 which will take them on a direct flight to the United States. *U.S. Air Force photo.*

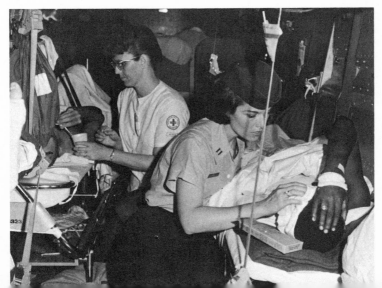

Sciences Corps. These officers are the dieticians, physical therapists and occupational therapists.

The Army and Navy each have Medical Departments to oversee their medical facilities and personnel. The Air Force has its counterpart, which is the Biomedical Sciences Corps. While these three medical components are part of their individual services, they each remain a separate department and have their own directors of nursing and medical specialists, separate from the directors of WACS, WAVES, and WAF. The doctors and dentists in the armed forces also come under the service's medical departments.

Everywhere a serviceman or woman is stationed there must be a medical facility. To man these facilities there must be doctors, dentists, nurses, dieticians, physical therapists, occupational therapists and their supporting medical personnel. Italy, Germany, Spain, Guam, Japan, England, Puerto Rico, Morocco, Thailand and Vietnam are just a few of the overseas assignments available.

The requirements for a commission in either the nursing or medical specialists corps are the same as those for the other distaff-line officers in the armed forces. There are slight variations between the services in the age limitations: in the Army, ages 20–33; in the Navy, ages 20–34; and in the Air Force, ages 20–35. The Navy and Air Force accept married nurses or medical specialists; however, they may not have dependents under eighteen years of age. All four services allow their female officers to marry after they have completed officer candidate training. Application for a commission is similar to that of the WAC, WAVE, Woman Marine and WAF. In addition to the basic officer requirements there are specialized educational achievements that must be met, such as being a graduate of an approved nursing school or possessing a baccalaureate degree qualifying one in a medical area. Some young women desiring to become nurses or dieticians cannot afford the educational expense. There are, however, assistance programs.

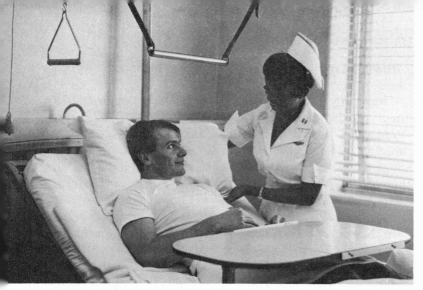

Air Force lieutenant nurse administers to the needs of a patient at Randolph Air Force Base hospital. *U.S. Air Force photo.*

NURSE CORPS

The Army, Navy, and Air Force each offer various financial assistance programs, which range from financial aid and officer commissions in either the junior or senior years of college, to a complete four-year program paid for by one of the services. For each of these individual financial aid programs there are different active duty obligations incurred. Some services require two years of active service as a nurse, and some require four. They are explained at the end of this chapter.

The Army sends its nurses to Brooke Army Medical Center, Fort Sam Houston, Texas, for eight weeks of orientation. At Fort Sam Houston the nurse learns not only Army routine, but military nursing. The Navy nurse attends eight weeks of orientation at Newport, Rhode Island. The Air Force sends its nurses to Sheppard Air Force Base, Texas, for their introduction to Air Force nursing.

ARMY NURSE

The Army nurse has four general fields open to her: direct nursing care, teaching, administration and supervision, and special assignments. Those in direct nursing care find themselves working in hospitals both in the United States and abroad, working as staff nurses in all of the clinical specialities, such as medical, surgical operating room, neuropsychiatric, child health, and maternity. Every nursing speciality is needed.

In the course of her career a nurse might be an instructor of a military nursing course at one of the Army's medical training centers or possibly a faculty member of the School of Nursing at the University of Maryland. In the administration field she could serve on the staff of the Army Surgeon General or be a nursing supervisor. Among the areas of special assignments are nursing researchers, recruiters, or advisors to military nurses of Allied nations.

A nurse in the surgical ward of a field hospital near Nha Trang, Vietnam, writes a letter for one of her patients. *U.S. Army photo.*

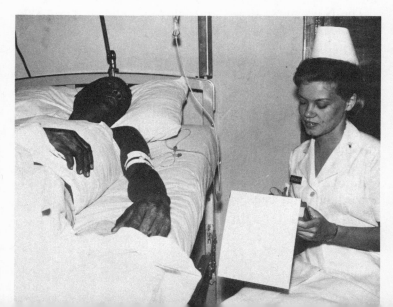

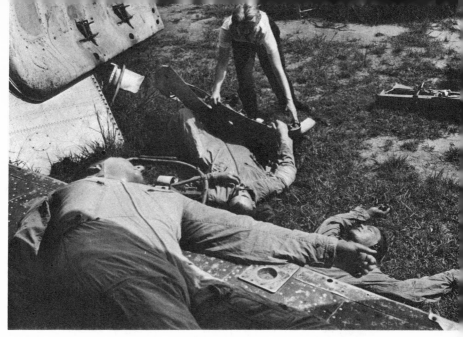

An Air Force nurse receives specialized training at a simulated plane crash. *U.S. Air Force photo.*

NAVY NURSE

The Navy nurse serves both on shore and at sea, caring for sailors and Marines. Often in her career she will serve both in the United States and in a foreign country. For example, she could be a staff nurse in San Diego, California, or a head nurse at Parris Island, South Carolina. She might be an instructor in nuclear nursing at Bethesda, Maryland, or serving at Bethesda Naval Hospital, caring for the President or head of a foreign nation who needs a serious operation that is beyond the capability of the medical facilities in his own country. The naval nurse's primary distinguishing feature from Army and Air Force nurses is assignments aboard hospital ships such as the U.S.S. *Sanctuary* and U.S.S. *Repose.*

AIR FORCE NURSE

The Air Force nurse may serve in forty-three of the fifty states and twenty-three foreign lands, such as Pakistan, Libya, Morocco, Okinawa, Spain, the Azores, Bermuda, England, Crete, Thailand and Vietnam. The Air Force has two unique fields of nursing, the aerospace and flight or "air evacuation" nurses.

A flight nurse must be a regular or career officer, not more than thirty-six years of age and medically accepted for flying before she may be trained as a flight nurse. These aspiring flight nurses must attend a six-week course at the School of Aerospace Medicine, Brooks Air Force Base, Texas. They are instructed in aviation physiology, psychology, in-flight patient care, and other subjects. After graduation they add wings to their uniform insignia. While flying they may wear more casual uniforms such as slacks, windbreakers and loafers. The flight nurse also draws flight pay, just like pilots and other aircrew members. This is additional pay to her regular checks. She is the "medical nursing authority" aboard the aircraft and all medical responsibilities are entrusted to her. For this reason flight nurses are alternated between airborne and ground assignments so they may keep abreast of the more recent nursing advances and techniques. This also enlarges the opportunities for flight nurses and the pool of experienced airborne nurses.

MEDICAL SPECIALISTS CORPS

The Medical Specialists Corps officers are those who are trained dieticians, physical therapists and occupational therapists. Their requirements for a commission are the same as those of a nurse.

The female officers of the Medical Specialists Corps attend basic indoctrination just as the nurses and other officers do. The Army Medical Specialists Corps indoctrination is held at Brooke Army Medical Center, Fort Sam Houston, Texas; the Navy at Newport, Rhode Island; and the Air Force at Sheppard Air Force Base, Texas.

After completing their orientation, the new officers are normally assigned to a stateside hospital. After a year of active duty they may apply for an overseas tour. Medical specialists serve in hospitals and clinics around the world.

THE SPECIALISTS

The *dietician* selects food, plans menus and restricted diets, and supervises the personnel who prepare the meals. She makes sure that the menus meet all the nutritional requirements for good health or medical recovery. Her job of revitalizing the bodies of thousands of patients in her care can become quite challenging when she is in charge of a hospital's food service in a foreign country where fresh fruits and vegetables may carry disease. She could also be part of a research program, planning astronauts' diets, or teaching others her skills.

The *occupational therapist* is guided by physicians in her job of rehabilitating mentally and physically disabled patients. She plans and supervises vocational, educational and recreational programs to help these people become self-sufficient. In addition to helping patients regain emotional and physical stability, her skills are used to alleviate boredom of patients with long-term illnesses. Her treatment program consists of both manual and creative efforts such as clay modeling, leather-working, weaving, and the manual skills of typing, business machine operation, and power tools. Her goal is to teach a patient not only the routines of daily living but to work toward an eventual return to employment.

The *physical therapist* is an expert with both her hands

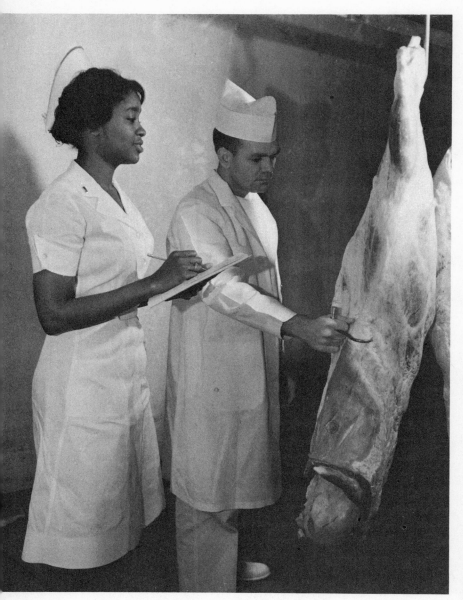

An Air Force dietitian inspects a side of beef. *U.S. Air Force photo.*

and machines in the art of restoring the functions of disabled parts of the body. Her patients are those with muscle, nerve, bone, and joint diseases or injuries. Under a physician's direction, she treats her patients through physical exercise, using mechanical apparatus, massage and applications of heat, cold, light, water or electricity. She takes muscle and nerve tests and keeps very accurate records as to the patient's rehabilitation. She also teaches her patients how to accept their handicaps, perform exercises, use and care of braces, crutches and artificial limbs. She may even instruct relatives on how to care for the patient at home.

As mentioned previously, the doctors and dentists also fall under these three medical departments. Requirements for a commission are the same as those of other medical service officers, but some enter the armed forces in a higher grade than second lieutenant. The initial rank is based upon experience.

EDUCATIONAL ASSISTANCE

ARMY

Students who are in their junior year in medical school are eligible for the Army Senior Medical Student Program. If selected for this program the student receives the pay and allowances of a commissioned officer while finishing his or her education and receiving the M.D. degree. Participants must agree to serve for three years of active duty after finishing their internship.

The Army Senior Veterinary Student Program is identical for the student working toward the D.V.M. degree. The obligation is to serve on active duty for three years after graduation.

Full-time student nurses who have completed the first two years in an approved school of nursing and are between

Two Navy medical officers aboard the U.S.S. *Repose* operate the Huggins cytoglomerator, a machine which reconstitutes frozen blood. *U.S. Navy photo.*

the ages of 18 and 28 may be accepted in the Army Student Nurse Program. Women must be single. The student is paid the salary and allowances of an E-3 rank (over $250 a month) for the last year of her studies. After receiving the diploma in nursing, there is an obligation to serve on active duty for two years.

There is also an Army Student Nurse Program for students enrolled in a four-year program leading to a degree. To be eligible, the student must have completed the first two years of nursing. Women must be single and between the ages of 18 and 28. For the first eighteen months the student receives the pay and allowances of an E-3 rank, and the pay of a second lieutenant ($550.68 per month) for the final six months of college. After receiving the cap, the student nurse must serve either two or three years of active duty, depending upon the amount of assistance received.

For those who would like to be Army dieticians there is the Army Student Dietician Program. Full-time students, 18 to 28 years of age, who have completed their sophomore year in home economics, majoring in food and nutrition or in institution management are eligible. If accepted the student draws the pay and allowances of the E-3 rank until graduation from an accredited college or university. The student is required to serve on active duty as a commissioned officer for two or three years, depending on the amount of assistance received.

There is also a program for the occupational therapist called Army Student Occupational Therapy Program. Students become eligible after completing their sophomore year in college and are enrolled in the curriculum of occupational therapy. Selectees receive the pay and allowances of a sergeant and after receiving their degree serve from two to three years as an officer, depending upon the assistance received.

For the girl who cannot financially manage even to dream about registering in a nursing school, the Army offers the "Walter Reed Army Institute of Nursing Program." A qualified applicant for this program attends her locally accredited college or university for the freshman and sophomore years and then she transfers to the University of Maryland for the remaining two years to finish training and receive her nursing degree.

NAVY

The Navy has a program for the student nurse called the Navy Nurse Corps Candidate Program. Nursing students, male or female, who have a high school education, are in their sophomore or junior year in a nursing school and will be within the age group of 20 to 29 upon graduation, are eligible. While finishing their nursing education the student receives tuition, books, room and board plus $99.37 a month until six months prior to completion of degree requirements. At this time the students are commissioned and begin drawing the salary of an ensign. The total enrollment is not to be longer than twenty-four months in this program. If assistance was received for twelve months or less there is a two-year active duty obligation. If the assistance was for more than twelve months the active duty period is three years.

The Navy has assistance for the medical student through its Navy Senior Medical Student Program. To be eligible the student must be enrolled in her junior year of study leading to a Doctor of Medicine degree. Until completion of his or her study the student receives the pay and allowances of a lieutenant junior grade of $628.10 per month. The graduate must serve on active duty for three years after graduation.

The Navy Dietician Internship Program is for men and women in the age group of 21 to 31½ who have a baccalaureate degree in foods and nutrition or institutional management. During the internship period the student receives the pay and allowances of a lieutenant junior grade. Males must serve for three years and women for two years plus a month for every month of financial assistance over twelve months.

Physical therapists are needed by the Navy and may participate in the Navy Physical Therapist Student Program. To be eligible, the student must be in the 21 to 31½ age group and within twelve months of completing an approved course in physical therapy leading to a baccalaureate degree. Males must serve three years; women for two years after completing their education. While in this program students receive a salary of a lieutenant junior grade.

The Navy Occupational Therapist Student Program takes applicants in the 21 to 31½ age group who are enrolled in an approved clinical occupational therapy training program. While finishing their education the students receive a salary of a lieutenant junior grade. After receiving the degree or certificate in occupational therapy the males must serve three years and women for two years.

AIR FORCE

Medical students interested in an Air Force career or wishing to serve in the flying service may become flight surgeons after receiving their medical degrees. Students who are in their junior year in medical school may be selected for the Air Force Senior Medical Student Program. While finishing their education they receive the pay and allowances of a second lieutenant and must serve for three years after receiving their medical degree.

The Air Force Dietetic Internship Program is open to students in the 21 to 26 age group who have a baccalaureate degree and have been accepted for internship. The Air

Force pays the student a second lieutenant's salary and allowances during internship. The dietetic internship includes a six-month residency at a selected Air Force hospital. The student must serve three years of active duty after finishing internship.

The Air Force Physical Therapist Student Program is open to eligible students between the ages of 21 and 26 years who are within twelve months of completing an approved course in physical therapy. During the final period of education the student receives a second lieutenant's pay and allowances. After receiving a degree the student must serve three years of active duty.

The Air Force Occupational Therapist Student Program is open to students who are between 21 and 28 years of age and are enrolled in an approved clinical occupation therapy program. They receive the pay and allowances of a second lieutenant while completing the requirements for a certificate or degree and then must serve for three years of active duty after termination of their schooling.

Thus, medical educational opportunities are found throughout the armed forces. It is up to the individual to take advantage of them.

CHAPTER 16

Education—Continuing to Grow

The armed forces are the largest educational institution in the world, not only in military schooling, but also in offering education in non-military courses. Through the facilities and programs in all of the military and naval services it is possible for someone to get a high school diploma and then progress on up to receive a doctor's degree. In some cases the armed forces will pay all of the tuition, in others 75 percent of the cost of the courses. For some, the student not only has all of the fees paid, but is also paid his or her normal salary and allowances.

It has often been said that military service is one long training school. Certainly to progress in any career a person must continue to learn in order to master new things and achieve success. For the young woman who has the desire, the opportunities for further education are unlimited.

Many colleges provide classes on the bases and one, the University of Maryland, claims to have the largest campus in the world. For example, this university has many professors assigned to teach classes at military bases in Europe. At Munich, Germany, it has a two-year college, which is attended by dependents of personnel stationed in Europe. The University of Southern California is another example. It offers courses leading to a graduate degree on air bases in Europe and in the Pentagon. Just about anywhere in the world there is a college campus away from home. Where there is not, an education center is available that arranges correspondence courses for the men and women stationed in the area.

Recognizing the value of education, the services have a Tuition Assistance Program to permit all personnel to take advantage of this schooling, in addition to the GI Bill.

All active duty servicemen and women except officers with less than two years to serve are eligible for tuition assistance. Up to 75 percent of the tuition fees for off-duty study at accredited schools will be paid by the Government. The only limitation is that not more than $14.25 per semester hour will be paid, which means the student must pay the remainder. The Coast Guard pays 100 percent of the fees. This tuition assistance is for studies leading to a bachelor and advanced degrees in recognized colleges and universities. Many of these colleges conduct classes on the military bases or the student commutes to the nearby campus for evening classes. There is no obligation for further service for enlisted personnel who take advantage of this free education.

Another unusual educational system in the armed forces is the USAFI—the United States Armed Forces Institute. The main office of the Institute is located at Madison, Wisconsin. The Institute supplies texts, testing booklets and the necessary forms to its campuses—bases, camps, posts, stations and ships at sea, which give USAFI courses during off-duty hours or through correspondence.

The enrollment fee is $5.00. Most of the courses are free. They range from the elementary school level up through the sophomore year in college. Thus a student who does not have a high school education could receive his diploma through USAFI, and if he or she wishes, continue on and obtain two years of college credit. These credits are accepted by more than 1,200 different colleges and universities in the United States and in some foreign countries.

All of the correspondence courses and some certain other tests are sent to the USAFI headquarters in Madison for grading and evaluating. It is here that a complete record is kept on the student. When the individual leaves the service a copy of the credits will be sent to the college the student has selected.

For those men and women who are willing to utilize the programs mentioned above, the armed forces offer another unusual opportunity to obtain their college degrees. In the Army and Air Force the program is unofficially called "Operation Bootstrap," which comes from the expression "raising oneself up by one's bootstraps." This literally means working one's way up the ladder. Once an individual has accumulated enough college hours through off-duty education, the armed forces will send that person on full salary and allowances to the college of his or her choice to complete the degree requirements. However, the student must pay the tuition and fees.

The Army requires that the student must be able to finish the degree requirements within one semester or two quarters. The Air Force will permit its personnel to go to a college for a short residence period to obtain his or her degree. Approximately 1,800 Air Force personnel each year are earning their degrees this way. Also under "Bootstrap," personnel may return to college for short periods to take courses related to their service jobs to improve their proficiency.

The Navy College Degree Program is offered to active-duty officers who can obtain a baccalaureate degree in twelve months or less through full-time attendance at a recognized college. The officer receives full pay and allowances, but must pay tuition and other expenses. In return for this schooling, the officer must agree to serve one year for each six months spent in this college program.

The Marine Corps offers a similar program to its officers who have sufficient credits to enable them to complete their degree requirements in a maximum of twenty-one months. Officers must agree to remain on active duty for three years beyond the completion of the program. The officer receives full pay and allowances while attending college, but must pay the tuition and other related expenses. The Marine Corps has an Advanced Degree Program.

Another unusual Army program offered for officers, in addition to "Operation Bootstrap," is called the Army Degree Completion Program. To be eligible an officer must have served three years of active duty and can complete his or her baccalaureate degree in one year or an advanced degree in six months of full-time attendance. The officer is required to serve on active duty for four years after graduation. In addition to giving the officer full salary and allowances, the Army pays tuition, fees and other expenses.

The Air Force offers educational advancement in technological, scientific and other professional areas for active duty personnel. These opportunities are at both the undergraduate, graduate and doctoral levels in the resident Air Force Institute of Technology at Wright-Patterson Air Force Base, Dayton, Ohio, and at selected universities. Officers selected under this program have all of their tuition and fees paid and receive full pay and allowances. The Navy conducts postgraduate courses of a similar nature at Monterey, California.

For enlisted personnel, only the Army, Navy, and Air Force have special degree programs in which personnel are sent to a college with all tuition and fees paid and receive their full pay and allowances. The Army has the unique Army Enlisted Schooling Program. In this case the Army assumes all costs for books, tuition, and other fees while continuing full pay and allowances to selected personnel who rate high scholastically. Students must take training that meets Army requirements. Enlisted personnel must extend their enlistment for three years for every year or less of schooling they take and for six years if the training requires more than one year of schooling.

To qualify for this higher education the serviceman or woman must be able to complete the training before age 35 and have a high school diploma or pass the General Educational Development Test.

A Yeoman Third Class at the Educational Services office at Whiting Field, Florida, explains the tuition aid program to an airman interested in furthering his schooling. *U.S. Navy photo.*

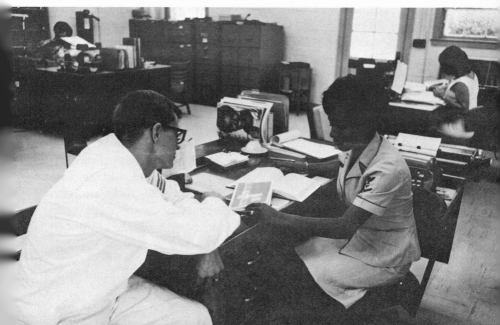

The Air Force has an Airman Educational Commissioning Program—AECP—for enlisted men and women who are carefully screened to determine if they have officer potential. These career-minded young men and women must have thirty semester hours of college credit before being considered. If selected, they are sent to an accredited college or university to obtain their baccalaureate degree. The Air Force, in addition to paying all fees and tuitions, keeps the individual on full pay and allowances. After receiving a degree, the individual then attends Officer Training School and must serve four years after being commissioned a second lieutenant.

The hard-working and studious WAVE and Woman Marine who is career-minded may also participate in a similar program, which is called the Navy Enlisted Scientific Education Program. Applicants must be 21 years of age or older for WAVES, but there is no age minimum for the Marines; have a high school education and compete in an annual examination. Those selected may receive up to four full years of college while drawing full pay and allowances. The Navy pays for the tuition, books and fees. Following graduation, the individual must complete Officer Candidate School and serve for four years on active duty.

Those members of the Armed Forces who wish a career in medicine have many unusual programs while in the service and even before finishing their schooling if they wish to serve in the armed forces for a full-time career or for only a short period of time. One example is the Navy enlisted hospital corps personnel in the grade of E-4 or above and who are high school graduates may enter the Navy Nurse Education Program. They receive full pay and allowances while attending an accredited nursing school. They may receive up to four years of education and then serve for four years on active duty from the date they enter Officer Candidate School.

MEDICAL SCHOOLING

In addition to the educational possibilities available for those inclined toward the liberal arts, business, scientific, and technical areas, there are equally great opportunities for those in the health field, especially nurses.

The Army offers these advanced clinical specialization courses: anesthesiology, 78 weeks; health nursing, 48 weeks; operating room nursing, 22 weeks; military nursing practice and research, 40 weeks; neuropsychiatric nursing, 24 weeks; nursing career course, 23 weeks; and health administration, 39 weeks. All except the last course are conducted in Army hospitals or at the Medical Field Service School, Brooke Army Hospital, Fort Sam Houston, Texas. The administrative course is taken at Baylor University in Texas and the student receives a master's degree.

The Navy has full-time and part-time enrollment plans for its nurses in university programs on the undergraduate and graduate level in nursing administration, education, research and related fields. While attending college the officer receives full pay and allowances and the Navy pays all tuition and fees. In addition, the Navy Nurse Corps in-service training programs prepare Navy nurses for advancement with an anesthesia program at Bethesda Naval Hospital in Washington, D.C., in collaboration with George Washington University; a management program at the U.S. Navy Postgraduate School, Monterey, California; plus six-month courses in orthopedic nursing and operating room nursing and a number of short courses in nursing, public health, administration and education.

The Air Force offers further education to its nurses through its Institute of Technology programs. In these the officer is sent to a civilian school to finish her degree requirements up through the doctoral level on full pay and allowances. In addition, the Air Force has a six-month advanced obstetrical nursing program, an eighteen-month anesthesia course, a six-month nursing service administration course, a six-week flight nurse course, and the most unusual nursing course in all of the armed forces—the aerospace nursing course. Each year two Air Force nurses receive special training and are assigned as nurses to the astronauts while the latter are at Cape Kennedy preparing for space flights. Along with special doctors, the two nurses are on hand for each launch to help maintain the health of the astronauts before the flight and to care for them when they return.

TRAINING IN TECHNICAL SPECIALTIES

With the rapid growth in knowledge and the need to keep current as new devices and techniques emerge out of man's quest for knowledge, a person receiving training in a technical field will soon find herself unable to understand or work on the new equipment that is constantly entering use in the armed forces. For example, a person trained originally in electronic equipment using tubes is unable to work on the new transistorized equipment without more training. The same is true of computers, jet engines and missiles, to mention but a few.

To keep its people current, the armed forces continually train them, either on the bases or at special training centers throughout the nation. Often men and women are sent to factories making new equipment to learn how to operate it when it is turned over to the Government. Thus, the armed services are truly a continuing education type of organization. For the lazy person who does not wish to continue learning it means an end to advancement. This is also true in civilian life, but in the armed forces this new education to keep one up-to-date on new developments in a speciality is paid for by the Government. In civilian life it usually means that the individual who wants to advance in his speciality must pay for his or her own further education and take the training in off-work periods of time. One of the reasons why men and women who have been trained in a speciality in the armed forces often have little difficulty in obtaining jobs when they leave the service is because the employer knows they are up-to-date in their training.

Management and the training of executives is a continuing effort in the armed forces. For the non-commissioned officer there are special schools that train and improve the individual's capability to lead. Attendance at one of these schools is coveted and selection is made on the potential of the individual for further growth.

For the officers there are also professional schools that prepare them for greater responsibility and higher positions. The Army has a Staff and Command College, the Navy has a War College, the Marine Corps has a Command and Staff College, and the Air Force has an Air War College for middle-ranking officers. For senior officers there is an Armed Forces Staff College, the Industrial College and the National War College. The latter two are located at Fort McNair in the District of Columbia and are also attended by high government civil servants and diplomats from the State Department. One of the opportunities for students at these colleges is that the courses they take are accepted for credit by such universities as George Washington, which awards a master's degree to the student if he takes certain courses at the University and submits a satisfactory thesis. For the officers there is also the opportunity to compete for a few openings at the Royal Air Force Staff College in England and the NATO College in Rome.

The armed forces recognize that if they are to continue to be able to deter war they must have the best-educated men and women in the world. To gain this, they offer a wide variety of opportunity for all personnel, both men and women. From there it is left to the individual, who early realizes that whether or not he or she intends to make the services a career or seek a career in civilian life, a person's earning power and chance for advancement is directly tied to the amount of education and training the individual has obtained. In a lifetime it can mean hundreds of thousands of dollars.

CHAPTER 17

The Service Life

One of the aims of the United States Government is to have all-volunteer armed forces so it will not have to depend on the draft for manpower. In 1970 a special presidential commission reported to the President the various ways that this could be accomplished. One of the possibilities considered was to increase the number of women in uniform. Among the various sources of information that this group, called informally the "Gates Commission," used were the numerous surveys that the armed forces frequently conduct to feel the pulse of its people.

One such survey by the Women of the Air Force is typical of those conducted by all the uniformed services. These were the facts learned by the WAF:

Over half of the officers are in their 20's.

A third of the enlisted WAF are 18 or 19, and over one half are in their 20's.

20 percent of the WAF are married and of these, 14 percent have Air Force husbands.

A third of the WAF entered the Air Force for travel and new experience. Almost half of the Airman Basics give that as the reason for enlisting.

A fourth of the WAF wanted to serve the nation or be involved in something worthwhile.

Another fourth thought that advancement opportunities, training, experience and education were their reasons for joining up.

Three-quarters of the WAF officers and three-fifths of the enlisted WAF are satisfied with their jobs.

An overwhelming majority of the WAF indicated they would like to have an overseas assignment.

The facts turned up by this survey pretty much speak for the WAC, WAVE, and Women Marines. Surveys tend to deal with numbers and percentages and often do not give the whole picture. Most people do things, such as enlist in the armed forces, for a variety of reasons.

Certainly the lure of travel, new friends and new experiences are strong reasons for a young woman to enlist. Fortunately she is able to combine these inducements with a patriotic desire to serve her nation and do something worthwhile. In doing so she receives training, job experience, further education and belongs to an organization where advancement is dependent on ability and desire to work.

Just what is service life and what does it require of a person? The commanding officer of a training center for women once said, "Military service is no life for a person who dislikes deviation from the routine or expected things. This kind of life requires adaptability, it requires flexibility. To be happy in it, an individual requires a bit of adventure in her spirit, a willingness to take in stride whatever comes along. She must be receptive toward new ideas, new situations, new ways of doing things."

WAFs in official evening uniforms. *U.S. Air Force photo.*

One of the first things that a young woman must understand before entering the ranks of the armed forces is that she is not only taking a job, she is embarking into a new way of life. She will be paid on an equal basis with men and have the same basic privileges. She will also have the same responsibilities and limitations.

For example, she must go where she is ordered and she must do as she is told. She may want to pack her bags and go home sometimes, but she cannot quit this job as she could a civilian job. She may have to work anywhere at any time and she may on occasions work long hours. Since she is on a fixed salary she will not be paid for overtime.

The commander of the training center also said: "Among career people in the services, there is a sense of dedication. It begins with the solemn swearing-in of the officer, or the oath of enlistment of the recruit. It continues all during service. From the first day of training, certain principles such as devotion to duty are repeated over and over again. The job must be done, regardless of when the clock says it is time to quit.

"The standards of performance that most career people set for themselves are such as to warrant the respect of their colleagues. The training of the officer to look after the welfare of the personnel for whom she is responsible is constant until it becomes second nature. This is not just any job, this is a special one for which that individual is vitally necessary. It is a feeling that is not confined to officers or non-commissioned officers. It goes all the way down to a new recruit, and helps to satisfy a deep-seated need in all of us to be useful."

Not every young woman, of course, is suitable for a career in uniform. The young woman who cannot adjust to a group situation is not going to remain in uniform very long. Yes, one can be fired from the armed forces!

PAY AND BENEFITS

What are the benefits of a service career? Personnel in the armed forces are paid a regular salary, depending upon rank and the amount of time served. The pay for a basic recruit is $124.50 per month. The highest pay for an enlisted woman is $903.60 per month, which she receives when she reaches the non-commissioned officer rank of Senior Master Sergeant in the Army and Air Force, Master Chief Petty Officer in the Navy and Sergeant Major in the Marine

Two Marines examine a fine silk kimono in a gift store in Koza, Okinawa. *Defense Dept. Photo* (*Marine Corps*).

Corps. In addition, everyone in uniform receives $48 per month for food and from $60 to $120 per month for rent if she does not live in government housing.

The officer pay scale starts at $577.20 per month for a second lieutenant and ensign and goes to $2,750.40 per month for a four-star general or admiral. Officers also receive the $48 per month for food and from $110 to $200 for housing if they do not occupy government housing.

Since men and women are paid equally by rank, their retirement programs are the same. The earliest one can retire is after twenty years of service. At this point they receive 50 percent of their pay for the remainder of their lives. If a person retires after thirty years they receive 75 percent of their pay. All active duty and retired personnel are permitted to shop at exchanges and ships' stores. These are well-stocked department stores and their prices are very low compared to prices in civilian stores.

All personnel receive $10,000 free life insurance and can buy another $10,000 for a small monthly premium. They receive free medical, dental and hospital care. All personnel, regardless of rank, receive thirty days of vacation with pay each year.

LIVING CONDITIONS

About the best description that can be given of housing and living conditions for enlisted women is to liken them to living in a college dormitory. Since group living is the rule in the armed forces, this means a barracks. But to think of it as similar to a cold and drafty wooden barracks that men lived in many years ago is creating the wrong picture. Today, the quarters are modern and comfortable. Single rooms are assigned to the highest ranking women, who have the same supervising responsibility as a college dormitory housemother. The lower ranks, as at college, usually share a room. This might be two or three women to a room. The furniture is not unlike that the young woman has at home in her own bedroom and the woman in uniform is given a lot of freedom in decorating her living area. If space permits she may even have her own television in her room.

Facilities in the barracks as a rule include sewing machines, hair dryers, ironing facilities, launderettes, kitchenettes and a comfortable lounge. This is like a living room and usually is furnished with a piano, hi-fi, and color television for relaxation. It is used for entertaining dates and other guests. In addition there is a club on every base for enlisted ranks, swimming pools, theaters, bowling alleys and other recreational facilities. There are dances, parties and tours arranged at the service clubs. Since the ratio of men to women at most bases runs greater than twenty to one, there are few wallflowers.

As in a college dormitory, there are shared chores, such

as answering the telephone and taking special duty. Enlisted personnel must clean their own living quarters and share in other housekeeping duties.

All meals may be taken in dining halls; if an individual prefers to eat at her club or snack bar she may; however, she must pay as she would in a civilian restaurant. If she lives in government quarters, this means she does not receive the $48 a month, but is furnished three meals a day, seven days a week.

In off-duty periods the woman in uniform is able to live much as she would in civilian life. Although the services take responsibility for their personnel, the real responsibility for an individual's off-duty activities and the hours she keeps is placed squarely on her shoulders. From the moment the young lady enlists she is called a "woman" and the armed forces expect her to be mature, responsible and to

WACs rest during a bicycle trip in the Tannas Mountains, Oberreifenburg, Germany. *U.S. Army photo.*

exercise self-discipline. If she keeps late hours that affect her job, inconveniences others in her barracks, or reflects unfavorably on her uniform and service, she can be disciplined. If she does not maintain the moral standards of her service she will be "kicked out" quickly and returned to civilian life.

When an individual enters the armed forces she does not lose her rights as an American citizen, but she does come under military law, which is not significantly different from civilian law. This Code of Military Justice is basically concerned with the law on military bases and in military life. It is much like the "company rules" in a civilian company or business. Should a member of the armed forces break a civilian law she is treated as any citizen and tried in a civilian court. If convicted and sentenced, she would, of course, be discharged from the armed forces.

WORKING LIFE

Everyone in uniform has a job, just as in any business. Like any business there are normal hours when most people work, but since national defense is a 24-hour day, 365-day business, there is some shift work. The men and women in uniform, however, normally work a nine-hour day with one hour of this time for lunch. The shift work for some jobs, such as communications, is required because of the need to be alert at all times and to have the organization that can respond to an attack on a moment's notice. Despite this, the vast majority of personnel work only five days a week. If there is a need to work on weekends they are given other days off.

There is usually little drill and marching after a woman finishes basic training. This only occurs those days when there is a parade or an inspection, because the modern armed forces have largely gotten away from the old drill

Women Marines sightseeing in Kintai District of Iwakuni City, Japan, take a break on the west end of Japan's famous Kintai Bridge. *Defense Dept. Photo* (*Marine Corps*).

routines of the past. Of course there are some military duties that have to be accomplished by all personnel and this sometimes requires working a half-day on Saturday, but this too is now infrequent. In an effort to make the armed forces an attractive career, the military services try to pattern their working hours and time off after those of a civilian organization.

The wearing of the uniform in peacetime is usually only required during working hours or on special duty. Women in the services, like other working women, dress as they please when off-duty. As an example of allowing individuality, the women in uniform are not "issued" lingerie, but purchase it themselves according to their individual tastes.

As in civilian life, each office has a boss and since the armed forces has been basically a male organization, the supervisor is usually a man. However, as women in uniform move higher in rank and show their capabilities they are becoming supervisors. Promotions are based primarily on how a woman does her job and the leadership potential she shows in directing the men and women who are under her.

In time a woman can progress up through the enlisted ranks to the highest non-commissioned officer rank. The services are always looking for leaders and if such a woman has a college degree she can be selected for officer candidate school. If she does not have a degree, but works in her off-duty time to take advantage of her educational opportunities, she can obtain her degree and then become a commissioned officer. The highest rank held by women until 1970 was that of full colonel or Navy captain. On May 15, 1970, President Nixon nominated two women to become generals in the U.S. Army. The door has now been opened for women to hold any rank in any of the services.

One of the great attractions to service life is the opportunity to change places of work, which many find they like. Normally, people in uniform transfer every three years, going to another base in the United States or to an overseas base, where they usually work in the same type of job. But many people change career fields if they find their interests lie elsewhere.

One of the wonderful things about life in the uniformed service is the comradeship and opportunity to make quick friends. During a service career the woman finds that she frequently runs into friends she served with at other bases. Every time she changes jobs or is transferred she gains another circle of friends, something that is lacking too often in a civilian career.

SOCIAL LIFE

In the armed forces a woman meets and serves with people, male and female, who are much like herself. They all have to take the same rigid tests to get into the Army, Navy, Marine Corps, or Air Force. They have much in common, especially the organization they belong to, and usually have common interests. The new friends come from a cross section of America, from the small towns and rural areas to large cities. This association broadens an individual. Experience has proven that even if the woman decides not to make the armed forces a lifetime career, just one enlistment makes her more cosmopolitan and aware of the world than the friends she left behind to enter the service.

Women Marines visiting the Polynesian Cultural Center, Laie, Hawaii. *Defense Dept. Photo (Marine Corps).*

There is not a shortage of men in the armed forces and the opportunity for dates is unlimited. The men, like the women, come from all over the United States and the woman finds she works side by side with them just as she did in high school or in a civilian job. Women are respected in the armed forces, not only for their ability to do a job, but also as women. The services stress beauty hints and grooming and go to great lengths to provide smart and attractive uniforms to keep the woman feminine.

With this supply of eligible young men it is not surprising that many WACs, WAVES, Lady Marines, and WAF marry servicemen. As the Air Force survey showed, some 20 percent of the WAF are married and 14 percent have Air Force husbands. The service takes it for granted that every young woman expects to marry eventually. The recruit is not permitted to marry during basic training, but after that she is free to marry. She may not leave the service until she has completed part of her enlistment. This obligation depends on the rules of her service and is generally determined by the amount of investment the Government has made in training the individual.

What about marriage to someone else in uniform? It is the policy of the armed services to assign husband and wife to the same base. If the husband is assigned to a combat area, and the wife cannot serve there, they must of course be separated. As for living arrangements, the services permit both to draw their food and housing allowances and seek off-base housing if none is available for them on the base.

TRAVEL AND RECREATION

The armed forces today are sometimes described as the largest coeducational organization in the world. They are also unrivaled in opportunities for travel and recreation.

A monument of coral and carved driftwood holds the attention of these Marines visiting Sea Life Park, Waimalo near Koko Head, Hawaii. *Defense Dept. Photo (Marine Corps).*

Overseas tours are available for the career-minded individual and with the thirty days of vacation with pay the woman in uniform can "see Europe" and other foreign lands. In a comparable civilian job this type of travel and exposure to other peoples and cultures would not be possible. On an overseas tour she will live in a foreign land for usually three years. She will have the opportunity to learn the language on the base to which she is assigned and to explore the land at her leisure. On her vacations she can go wherever she pleases throughout the world. As a member of the armed forces she can get free rides on military aircraft and special fares on commercial flights. Jet travel puts the world a few hours away from her base.

In the United States, as well as overseas, the bases she is stationed on are like little cities; however, she has facilities she usually does not have in civilian life. For example, each base has a club for her use, a swimming pool, a bowling alley, sometimes a golf course, and a Special Services office that runs a number of recreation projects, such as picnic areas or clubs that teach her to fly an airplane or ride a horse. If she likes hobbies, the materials are available either free or at greatly reduced prices and the clubs offer instructions.

On each base is a chapel because the military services do not neglect the spiritual needs of its people. Chaplains of the Protestant, Catholic, and Jewish faiths are in uniform. They not only provide religious services, but also serve as counselors and administer to their flocks just like their civilian counterparts.

THE UNIFORM

Service life is "special" and the uniform makes it special. A Defense Department brochure has this to say:

"The first time a woman in the Service dons her uniform, something happens—she straightens up, holds her head high, proud to be a member of the military. Throughout basic training she is taught to wear her uniform with honor and pride. Perhaps this is unnecessary; for, almost instinctively, every servicewoman knows that in her uniform she is conspicuous, almost "special." She knows she's expected to be a model of behavior, and tends to refrain from doing things which would attract other than favorable attention, because she realizes the reflection would be not on herself as upon the Service whose uniform she wears."

It is this added something—this feeling of belonging, of contributing—that makes service life so alluring. Opportunity for travel, the pay, the benefits, the educational and training opportunities are all attractions, but the gratification of serving in an honorable and dignified profession becomes, after a number of years, of equal if not of greater importance to the individual.

CHAPTER **18**

Armed Forces Careers
and the Future

Although there is more and more of a trend for
women to have careers in the business and professional
world, a woman's natural instincts are for a home and family. Whatever a woman's job, whether in an office, a nursing
position in the professional world or as a research chemist,
she never loses that instinct. Some people refer to it as the
"nesting instinct," but however it is described it is a powerful and motivating force in the life of a woman.

The armed forces recognize this and, while they hope
that many of the women who don a uniform will choose it
as their life's work, they also understand and respect this
desire for a husband, children and a home. Unfortunately,
pregnancy in uniform means automatic retirement but some
visualize a day when military women will be authorized
maternity leave. As mentioned before, there are many

married couples in the services. Many women marry servicemen and although they themselves are no longer in uniform, live a service life as their husbands are transferred from base to base. If the uniformed woman marries someone not in the service, the training and discipline she receives better prepares her for the future as a wife and mother. Also, the leadership training she gains while in uniform will make her a better member of the civilian community in which she lives. Her travel and exposure to a vast swath of people from all over the United States gives her a certain cosmopolitan air that makes her stand out among her new circle of friends. She becomes a distinct asset to her husband as he climbs the ladder in his chosen career. Her children benefit from her past experience as she leads them into adulthood.

A grateful government also continues to reward her for her contributions, whether she is single or married. For example, there is a continued opportunity for further training and education. Since World War II there have been a series of "GI Bills" which provide allowances for those who leave the service and wish to finish their education. These benefits also can be used before the individual leaves the service.

EDUCATION

Veterans' Readjustment Benefits Acts provide monthly payments for periods of time a veteran attends a recognized school, whether full-time or part-time. At present, a single veteran receives $175 a month while going to college full-time. These benefits are received only by people who served during a war or in a national emergency.

Using these benefits, a veteran can take an approved course at a university or college, at a vocational, trade, technical, business or correspondence school. There is also an approved cooperative program in which the training phase supplements the school phase. Farm cooperative training is one of the categories approved for eligible veterans under the GI Bill.

For the individual who wishes to take an approved apprenticeship training or training on-the-job, the GI Bill will pay the individual a reduced amount each month, which is less than that of the college student. This is because the college student under the GI Bill must pay the tuition out of the money she receives from the Veterans Administration. Regardless of the wages paid by the employer in the apprenticeship program, the Veterans Administration will pay a minimum allowance of $80 a month for a single person.

Also available is flight training, if the veteran has a private pilot's license. With this training the veteran can obtain a transport pilot's license and seek work with an airline, although as yet none of the major airlines in the United States have hired women pilots.

The maximum period of training is thirty-six months, but only the months spent in school count. The number of months is based on the number of months served. Thus a three-year enlistment provides thirty-six months of training. Since the normal college year is nine months this means it is possible for a veteran to obtain a degree if eligible for the GI Bill.

EMPLOYMENT BENEFITS

Veterans who do not serve more than four years have reemployment rights with their former employer. They have ninety days to reapply for their old job. For those who did not have a job before entering the armed forces and would like to receive training in a field other than the one they worked in while in uniform, the Department of Defense instituted Project Transition in 1967. Under this program servicemen are trained for a job in the final months of their service period.

Former employees of the Government have the same reemployment rights as one does who wants to return to his old civilian job. Furthermore, veterans are given preference in applying for Civil Service positions. A veteran has five points added to any grade received when taking an examination. Disabled veterans and holders of the Purple Heart Medal receive ten points. The training received in the armed forces is also credited toward experience requirements for Federal jobs. Many state, city and local governments also offer certain employment preferences to veterans.

These veterans who are unable to find employment immediately after release from active duty are entitled to unemployment insurance benefits based on the period of duty. The amount of benefits vary with each state.

LIFE INSURANCE AND DISABILITY BENEFITS

The $10,000 life insurance program a servicewoman is able to purchase for a small premium while on active duty is available when leaving the service. The veteran has 120 days in which to decide whether or not to continue this program as a civilian. Another $10,000 policy is available for larger premiums. So it is possible to have a $20,000 insurance estate started at relatively low premiums when leaving the armed forces.

If the servicewoman receives an injury while in uniform and it is disabling, she is retired. However, if the injury is not serious enough to disable her completely, it may be disabling to the extent that it affects her ability to work as well as she did before coming on active duty. If so, the Veterans Administration will, if the physical examination indicates this, pay the veteran a disability compensation—a monthly tax-free payment to those with disease or injury incurred in, or aggravated by military service. If the disability appears years after release from active duty the veteran is still eligible to receive a pension.

In addition to monthly payments, the disabled are eligible for vocational rehabilitation training, even if the disability shows up years later. All expenses for this training are paid by the Government.

Care in veterans hospitals is available to all veterans who have a disability. For those who do not have any disability connected with their service career, hospital care is available if the individual is not able to pay for treatment in a civilian hospital. The veteran is also eligible for outpatient medical and dental treatment if disabled, and care in domiciliary units and nursing homes. Another benefit is free prosthetic devices, such as artificial limbs, eyes, crutches, canes, and wheelchairs.

Unless the veteran is retired he or she is not entitled to care in armed forces hospitals. However, a woman service member who is pregnant when she leaves active duty is eligible to have her baby in an armed forces hospital.

LOANS FOR VETERANS

Eligible veterans and service members on active duty can obtain GI loans made by private lenders for the purchase of homes and farms. The Veterans Administration guarantees, insures, or makes direct loans. This usually ensures that the veteran can obtain the money needed at reduced interest rates. The Federal Housing Administration (FHA) also gives special preference to veterans in obtaining loans for the purchase or building of a home and the purchase of a farm.

SOCIAL SECURITY AND OTHER BENEFITS

On January 1, 1957, members of the armed forces became covered by the retirement, survivors' and disability insurance on a contributory basis. During the period of active service the woman in uniform has been contributing just as she would had she been working on a civilian job. The Government in turn has made the required contribution that a civilian business firm would make. The Social Security Program offers four kinds of protection and benefits: retirement, survivor, disability and medical. Once a person has worked ten years and contributed to the program she is eligible for life for these benefits.

In addition to the Social Security benefits, there are others that come to the survivors of a veteran upon his or her death. These are established by law and administered by the Veterans Administration. Certain assistance is also available to the survivors of veterans. Up to $250 can be paid toward a veteran's burial expenses if the veteran served during wartime or had a service-connected injury. All veterans are eligible to be buried in a national cemetery if they were honorably discharged. The Government will provide a flag for the casket and conduct a military ceremony.

SEPARATION FROM THE ARMED FORCES

Should the WAC, WAVE, Marine, or WAF decide not to continue her service career, at the end of enlistment she will receive full pay and allowances due her, plus pay for the days of leave not taken. A service member will not be paid for more than sixty days of leave. At the time of separation the veteran receives a travel allowance computed on the number of miles from the point of separation to the point where the member enlisted. This money is paid at the time of separation, or if the veteran is overseas when separation time comes she is transported to a base in the United States and then given the travel allowance.

REENLISTMENT

Depending on the branch of the armed forces and the types of skills, reenlistment rates sometimes run as high as 50 percent. Since the Government has spent considerable money and time in training its members it would like to retain all of them. By offering reenlistment bonuses (up to $10,000), which are based on the number of years in service, a woman in uniform can find herself with a bonus of several thousands of dollars plus a steady job for another three or four years if she decides to stay in uniform. Further training is available, in addition to more travel and more privileges as she progresses up the ranks.

THE FUTURE

Should she not elect to remain in uniform, the service-woman will be a much richer person and prepared to assume a career in the civilian world or that of marriage, children and a home. The odds are that sometime in the future she will work, whether as a single woman, a widow, a divorcee, or as a working wife. The floodgates of opportunity have opened for women.

WAC OFFICER CAREER FIELDS

Title
General Officer
Student Officer
Secretary of the General Staff
Congressional Liaison Officer
Major Departmental Unit, Chief
  or Director
Aide-de-Camp
Adjutant or Adjutant General
Administrative Officer
Nontactical Unit Officer
WAC Staff Adviser
Operations and Training Staff
  Officer
Research and Development Co-
  ordinator
Personnel Officer
Personnel Management Officer
Personnel Staff Officer
Manpower Control Officer
Recruiting and Induction Officer
ADPS Plans and Operations
  Officer
School Commandant
Assistant Professor of Military
  Science
Training Officer
Management Analyst
Training Center Unit Officer
Logistics Officer
Military College Faculty Mem-
  ber
Comptroller

Headquarters Unit Commander
General Supply Officer
Supply Staff Officer
Quartermaster Staff Officer
Subsistence Officer
Supply and Service Officer
Supply Management Officer
Army Exchange Officer
Procurement Officer
Special Services Officer
Army Band Officer
Information Officer
Finance and Accounting Officer
Finance Staff Officer
Finance Disbursing Officer
Budget and Fiscal Officer
Statistician
Legal Officer
Judge Advocate or Judge Advo-
  cate General
Civil Government Officer
Civil Affairs Staff Officer
Operations Research Systems
  Analysis
Military Intelligence Officer
Combat Intelligence Staff Officer
Psychological Warfare Officer
Installation Intelligence Officer
Strategic Intelligence Officer
Inspector General
Translation Officer
Interpreter
Intelligence Research Officer

WAC ENLISTED CAREER FIELDS

General Electronic Maintenance
  Field Communications Equip-
    ment Maintenance
  Teletypewriter Repairman
  General Cryptographic Re-
    pairman

Fixed Plant Communications
  Equipment Maintenance

  Fixed Station Attendant
  Fixed Station Receiver Re-
    pairman

Fixed Station Transmitter Repairman
Fixed Station Technical Controller
Fixed Plant Carrier Repairman
Fixed Ciphony Repairman
Fixed Cryptographic Equipment Repairman

Data Processing Equipment Maintenance
Tabulating Equipment Repairman
ADP Auxiliary Equipment Repairman
ADP Repairman

Precision Maintenance Precision Devices
Projector Repairman
Surveillance Photographic Equipment Repairman
Office Machine Repairman

Prosthetic Appliances
Cast Specialist
Brace Specialist
Dental Laboratory Specialist
Optical Laboratory Specialist

Textile and Leather Repair
Textile and Leather Repair Apprentice
Textile Repairman
Canvas Repairman
Shoe Repairman

Motor Transport
Light Vehicle Driver
Truckmaster

CLERICAL

Clerk
Administration
Clerk-Typist

Stenographer
Legal Clerk
Court Reporter
Postal Clerk
Medical Records Specialist
Personnel Specialist
Administrative Specialist
Movements Specialist
Flight Operations Coordinator
Information Specialist
Broadcast Specialist
Attache Specialist

Communications Center Operations
Communications Center Specialist
Telephone Switchboard Operator
Cryptographic Center Specialist

Finance
Pay Disbursing Specialist
Accounting Specialist
Finance Operations NCO

Data Processing
Data Processing Equipment Operator
Card and Tape Writer
Personnel Accounting Specialist
Machine Accounting Specialist
ADPS Console Operator
ADPS Programing Specialist
Assistant Systems Analyst

Supply
Supply Clerk
Engineer Supply and Parts Specialist
Ordnance Supply and Parts Specialist
QM Supply Specialist

QM Parts Specialist
Signal Supply and Parts
  Specialist
Transportation Supply and
  Parts Specialist
Medical Supply and Parts
  Specialist
General Supply Specialist
Film Library Specialist

GRAPHICS

Drafting and Cartography

General Draftsman
Construction Draftsman
Cartographic Draftsman
Map Compiler
Illustrator
Model Maker

Surveying

Topographic Computer

Printing

Process Photographer
Platemaker

Pictorial

Still Photographer
Motion Picture Photog-
  rapher
Audio Specialist
TV Production Specialist
Photographic Laboratory
  Specialist

GENERAL TECHNICAL

Medical Care and Treatment

Medical Corpsman
Medical Specialist
Clinical Specialist
Operating Room Specialist
Dental Specialist
Neuropsychiatric Specialist
Social Work/Psychology
  Specialist
Physical Therapy Specialist
Physical Reconditioning
  Specialist

Occupational Therapy
  Specialist
Electroencephalograph
  Specialist
EKG-BMR Specialist
X-Ray Specialist
Pharmacy Specialist
Food Inspection Specialist
Preventive Medicine
  Specialist
EENT Specialist

Laboratory Procedures

Medical Laboratory Spe-
  cialist
Petroleum Laboratory
  Specialist
Chemical Laboratory
  Specialist

*Technical Equipment
Operation*

Air Traffic Controller
Flight Simulator Specialist
Meteorological Observer
Microbarograph Specialist

Food Service

Food Service Apprentice
Cook
Baker
Hospital Mess Steward
Food Services Supervisor

Law Enforcement

Military Policeman
Assistant Criminal In-
  vestigator

General Intelligence

Intelligence Analyst
Interrogator
Image Interpreter

Special Intelligence

Military Intelligence
  Specialist
Military Intelligence
  Coordinator

Signal Intelligence
Cryptanalytic Specialist
Traffic Analyst
Voice Interceptor
Voice Countermeasures
Operator
Electronic Warfare
Operator-Analyst
Recruiter and Career
Counselor

Special Requirements
Electrical-Electronic En-
gineering Assistant
Mechanical Engineering
Assistant
Civil Engineering Assistant
Mathematics-Statistics
Assistant
Physical Sciences Assistant
Chemical Engineering
Assistant
Biological Sciences As-
sistant
Personnel Psychology
Specialist
Audit Specialist

Bandsman
Coronet or Trumpet Player
Baritone or Euphonium
Player

French Horn Player
Trombone Player
Tuba Player
Flute or Piccolo Player
Oboe Player
Clarinet Player
Bassoon Player
Saxophone Player
Percussion Player
Piano Player

Special Services
Entertainment Specialist
Physical Activities Spe-
cialist
Arts and Crafts Specialist
Recreation Supervisor

Linguists
Translator-Interpreter
Expert Linguist

Radio Code
Radio Operator
Radio Teletypewriter
Operator
Special Indentification
Operator
Communication Security
Specialist
Morse Interceptor
Teletypewriter Interceptor

WAF OFFICER CAREER FIELDS

Director of Personnel Manage-
ment
Director of Materiel
Comptroller
Planning & Programming Officer
Computer Systems Program-
ming Officer
Open Mess Secretary
Air Traffic Control Staff Officer
Weapons Controller

Space Systems Analyst
Space Sensor Systems
Audio-Visual Staff Officer
TV Production Officer
Motion Picture Production
Officer
Weather Officer
Advance Weather Officer
Chemist
Physicist

Mathematician
Research Officer Nuclear
   Weapons
Behavioral Scientist Personnel
   Measurement Psychologist
Scientist, Special
Electronics Engineer
Development Engineer, Special
System Program Staff Officer
Communications-Electronics
   Staff Officer
Communications Officer
Ground Electronics Officer
Electronic Computer Mainte-
   nance Officer
Transportation Staff Officer
Transportation Officer
Supply Services Staff Officer
Supply Services Operation
   Officer
Supply Services Sales Officer
Food Services Officer
Supply Management Staff
   Officer
Procurement Officer
Logistics Staff Officer
Logistics Officer
Accounting and Finance Officer
Budget Officer

Data Automation Staff Officer
Data Automation Officer
Management Analysis Staff
   Officer
Management Analysis Officer
Administrative Staff Officer
Administrative Officer
Personnel Staff Officer
Personnel Officer
Personnel Services Officer
Manpower and Organization
   Management Staff Officer
Management Engineering
   Officer
Education and Training Staff
   Officer
Education and Training Officer
Instructor
Information Staff Officer
Information Officer
Intelligence Staff Officer
Signals Intelligence Officer
Intelligence Photo-Radar
   Officer
Intelligence Officer
Air Targets Officer
Special Investigations Officer
Legal Staff Officer
Legal Officer

WAF AIRMAN CAREER FIELDS

First Sergeant
Intelligence
Photomapping
Audio-Visual
Weather
Aerospace Control Systems
   Operations
Communications Operations
Communications-Electronics
   Systems
Training Devices

Wire Communications Systems
   Maintenance
Intricate Equipment Mainte-
   nance
Aircraft Maintenance
Vehicle Maintenance
Civil Engineering Structural/
   Pavements
Fabric, Leather, and Rubber
Transportation
Supply Services

Food Service
Supply
Procurement
Accounting and Finance, and
   Auditing
Data Systems
Management Analysis
Administrative
Printing
Information
Personnel
Special Services

Education and Training
Band
Special Investigations and
   Counter-Intelligence
Medical
Dental
Officer Trainees
Unclassified Airmen
Recruiting
Military Training Instructors
Basic Trainees

WAVE OFFICER CAREER FIELDS

Meteorology
Oceanography
Intelligence
Computer Programming
Data Processing
Communications
Engineering
Public Relations
Legislative Liaison

Administration
Personnel Management
Personnel Planning
Education and Training
Finance
Merchandising
Comptrollership
Logistics
Supply

WAVE ENLISTED CAREER FIELDS

Aerographer's Mate
Radioman
Electronics Technician
Yeoman
Personnelman
Photographer's Mate
Disbursing Clerk
Hospital Corpsman
Dental Technician
Journalist
Air Controlman

Storekeeper
Aviation Storekeeper
Aviation Electronics Technician
Illustrator Draftsman
Data Processing Technician
Communications Yeoman
Aviation Maintenance Admin-
   istrationman
Data Processing Technician
Tradevman (Training Aids &
   Training Devices)

WOMEN MARINE CAREER FIELDS

Women Marines, officers and enlisted unless otherwise indicated, are serving in the following occupational or career fields:

Personnel and Administration
Intelligence
Logistics (Enlisted only)
Drafting and Surveying
(Enlisted only)
Lithography (Enlisted only)
Armament Repair (Enlisted only)
Operational Communications
Telecommunications Maintenance (Enlisted only)
Supply Administration and Operations
Transportation
Food Services
Auditing, Finance & Accounting
Data Processing
Marine Corps Exchange
Informational Services
Legal (Officers only)
Photography
Training Aids (Officers only)
Avionics
Air Control/Anti-Air Warfare
Aerology
Aviation Operations

MONTHLY PAY RATE AS OF 1 JULY 1969

Pay Grade	Qtrs Allow/6/	2 or less	Over 2	Over 3	Over 4	Over 6	Over 8	Over 10	Over 12	Over 14	Over 16	Over 18	Over 20	Over 22	Over 26
Commissioned Officers—See Notes 1, 2, 3, 4															
O-10	$201.00	$1,810.20	$1,874.10	$1,874.10	$1,874.10	$1,874.10	$1,945.80	$1,945.80	$2,094.90	$2,094.90	$2,244.90	$2,244.90	$2,394.60	$2,394.60	$2,544.30
O-9	201.00	1,604.40	1,646.40	1,681.80	1,681.80	1,681.80	1,724.10	1,724.10	1,795.80	1,795.80	1,945.80	1,945.80	2,094.90	2,094.90	2,244.90
O-8	201.00	1,453.20	1,496.70	1,532.40	1,532.40	1,532.40	1,646.40	1,646.40	1,724.10	1,724.10	1,795.80	1,874.10	1,945.80	2,024.10	2,024.10
O-7	201.00	1,207.20	1,289.70	1,289.70	1,289.70	1,347.00	1,347.00	1,425.30	1,425.30	1,496.70	1,646.40	1,759.80	1,759.80	1,759.80	1,759.80
O-6	170.10	894.60	983.40	1,047.60	1,047.60	1,047.60	1,047.60	1,047.60	1,047.60	1,083.30	1,254.30	1,318.50	1,347.00	1,425.30	1,546.20
O-5	157.50	715.50	840.90	898.20	898.20	898.20	898.20	926.10	975.60	1,040.70	1,118.70	1,182.90	1,218.30	1,261.20	1,261.20
O-4	145.05	603.60	734.40	783.90	783.90	798.00	833.70	890.40	940.50	983.40	1,026.30	1,054.80	1,054.80	1,054.80	1,054.80
O-3	130.05	561.00	627.00	669.60	741.60	776.70	804.90	848.10	890.40	912.00	912.00	912.00	912.00	912.00	912.00
O-2	120.00	449.70	534.00	641.40	662.70	676.50	676.50	676.50	676.50	676.50	676.50	676.50	676.50	676.50	676.50
O-1	110.10	386.40	427.80	534.00	534.00	534.00	534.00	534.00	534.00	534.00	534.00	534.00	534.00	534.00	534.00
Commissioned Officers who have been credited with over 4 years active service as enlisted members:															
O-3	130.05				$741.60	$776.70	$804.90	$848.10	$890.40	$926.10					
O-2	120.00				662.70	676.50	698.10	734.40	762.90	783.90					
O-1	110.10				534.00	570.30	591.60	612.90	634.20	662.70					
Warrant Officers—See Notes 1, 2, 3, 4															
W-4	$145.05	$571.20	$612.90	$612.90	$627.00	$655.20	$684.00	$712.50	$762.50	$798.00	$826.50	$848.10	$876.30	$905.40	$975.60
W-3	130.05	519.30	563.40	563.40	570.30	577.20	619.50	655.20	676.50	698.10	719.10	741.60	769.80	798.00	826.50
W-2	120.00	454.80	491.50	491.50	506.30	534.00	563.40	584.70	605.70	627.00	648.60	669.60	690.90	719.10	719.10
W-1	110.10	378.90	434.70	434.70	470.70	491.70	513.00	534.00	555.90	577.20	598.50	619.60	641.40	641.40	641.40
Enlisted Members—See Notes 1, 2, 3, 5, 6															
E-9	$120.00							$648.90	$663.90	$679.20	$694.20	$709.50	$723.60	$761.70	$835.80
E-8	120.00						$544.50	559.80	574.50	589.80	604.60	619.00	634.50	672.00	746.40
E-7	114.90	$342.30	$358.20	$372.90	$388.20	$455.40	469.80	484.80	500.40	522.60	537.30	552.30	559.80	597.30	672.00
E-6	110.10	294.90	313.30	328.80	343.20	385.70	433.20	433.20	455.40	469.80	484.80	492.60	492.60	492.60	492.60
E-5	105.00	254.70	283.50	305.70	328.80	365.70	380.70	395.70	410.10	417.90	417.90	417.90	417.90	417.90	417.90
E-4	Note 5	214.20	268.50	283.50	305.70	321.00	321.00	321.00	321.00	321.00	321.00	321.00	321.00	321.00	321.00
E-3	Note 5	155.10	216.30	231.30	246.30	246.30	246.30	246.30	246.30	246.30	246.30	246.30	246.30	246.30	246.30
E-2	Note 5	127.80	179.10	179.10	179.10	179.10	179.10	179.10	179.10	179.10	179.10	179.10	179.10	179.10	179.10
E-1	Note 5	123.30	163.80	163.80	163.80	163.80	163.80	163.80	163.80	163.80	163.80	163.80	163.80	163.80	163.80

NOTES:

1. Quarters allowance shown is for member with dependents.

2. Family separation allowance (FSA II) is $30 per month for members in grade E-4 over 4 years and above w/deps.

3. Hostile fire pay is $60 per month.

4. Subsistence allowance for officers and warrant officers is $47.88 per month.

5. Quarters allowance:

E1, E2, E3 =	$60.00 w/1 dep
	90.60 w/2 deps
	105.00 w/3 or more deps
E4 under 4 years =	90.60 w/1 or 2 deps
	105.00 w/3 or more deps
E4 over 4 years =	105.00 w/1 or more deps

6. Foreign Duty Pay:

E1, E2	$ 8.00
E3	9.00
E4	13.00
E5	16.00
E6	20.00
E7, E8, E9	22.50

Index